MW01294431

The Fight

Becoming Victorious in Any Situation

Sammy Spina

outskirts
press

Outskirts Press, Inc.
http://www.outskirtspress.com

Paperback ISBN: 978-1-9772-4852-7
Hardback ISBN: 978-1-9772-5096-4

Library of Congress Control Number: 2021921289

Cover designed by Cameron Cooper
Cover & interior images © 2022 Samuel J. Spina. All rights reserved - used with permission.

Outskirts Press and the "OP" logo are trademarks belonging to Outskirts Press, Inc.

PRINTED IN THE UNITED STATES OF AMERICA

Praising The FIGHT :

"Sammy has worked with me for more than 7 years now and continues to FIGHT through one of the most competitive industries in the world each day. I was with Sammy during a lot of his stories in THE FIGHT and watched how he handled these adversities first hand, relying heavily on his faith. I highly recommend this book to anyone who is experiencing self-doubt, a hard time, or just needs some extra motivation in their life."

Ralph Stringer –
Founder & President of Neostar Football

"Sammy is a hard-working, blue-collared Pittsburgh guy. His faith, dedication, and persistence has led him to not only become a great athlete agent, but also a trusted friend."

Dan Marino -
Pro Football Hall of Fame Quarterback

"Sammy is a talented, driven guy who won't let anything stand in the way of his success ... or the success of his clients. As a former athlete, I have a true appreciation for someone who is driven to be great and FIGHTs for what they believe in."

Jason Taylor -
Pro Football Hall of Fame Defensive End

"Very motivating and educative. The Fight guides readers on how helpful it is to have a positive mindset in the face of adversity; and even when being told 'no.' Using personal experiences, the author encourages readers on how to face bad circumstances head on with optimism, persistence and hard work. It is one that readers can draw inspiration from. I recommend."

Jessica Raymond -
Professional Editor

DEDICATION:

To my father, Samuel Spina. I love you more than words can describe. You have and will always be there for me. I think about you and miss you every single morning when I open my eyes. You truly are my hero. RIP Big Guy!

Samuel Spina
November 13, 1962 – March 20, 2017

Table of Contents

Acknowledgments

First, thank you *Jesus Christ*, my Lord and Savior, for all that You have done in my life. You've made the impossible, possible. You've opened doors and paths that I didn't even know existed. You are my everything.

Mom, I love you; you're my rock! Thank you for all of the sacrifices that you continue to make for our family! You are my role model. You have always put your selfish desires aside to take care of me and Mara. Thank you for everything.

Mara, I'm very proud of you. You have grown into an amazing young woman and I'm excited to watch your life continue to unfold. Thank you for being the best little sister that a big brother could ask for.

Nick Cupari & Kory Imbrescia – I'm not sure where I would be without you two. You've been with me since the beginning, and I consider you my brothers. I love you guys! Thank you for helping me stay out of trouble and keeping me on the right path.

Ralph Stringer – thank you for everything you've done in my life. You're a huge inspiration and have been by my side during some extremely difficult times. I'm honored to call you family and to have you as a mentor. I've spoken with you every single day (multiple times a day) since my father's passing. Thank you for always being there.

Tanner Lakey – thank you for helping me rediscover our Lord and Savior, Jesus Christ. You're my brother for life. I'm super grateful for you, my man. I truly don't know where I would be at in my life without you.

Cameron Cooper – My little brother! Thank you for being you bro. I am super proud of everything you have already accomplished and I know the future is extremely bright for you! By the way, you designed one heck of a cover for this book! Thank you.

Vinnie Scirotto – my ride or die! You've sacrificed a ton and have believed in the vision since the beginning! It's been a lot of fun my brother. A lot of sleepless nights, but thank you for always being there. We're just getting started.

Jordan Levinson – You're an inspiration to me every day. I've learned a ton from you… more than you are aware of. You have shown me things that I didn't believe to be attainable. Shoot, you've shown me things that I didn't know existed. I honestly don't know where I would be today if God didn't put you, Mark Bryn, and your family into my life.

Geno McCourt, Samuel Rony, Dan Marino, Jason Taylor, Seth Levit, my entire Downtown Squad, Krystal Vargas, and all of my friends who I consider family, THANK YOU. You have all helped make this journey possible.

1. Discover Yourself

2020 HAS BEEN a difficult year. We've been faced with adversity on a global scale like never before. I get it... it's tough. There's no way of hiding that. Countless people have lost their jobs. Countless more have lost family members, friends, and other loved ones to COVID-19. Bills are stacking up, rents due, emotions are running wild, anxiety is at all all-time high, and nobody seems to have a clear-cut answer on what we should do. Honestly, I don't know if anyone has the answer. What I do know is that we can only control so much in life. We can't let those things that are out of our control, like COVID-19, completely disrupt us or shut us down ... physically, emotionally, or spiritually.

We experience many positive and negative moments in life. We can feel untouchable one day, and then on the next, like the world is closing in on us. That, in essence, is what makes us human. We are very emotional creatures and we act on our emotions far too often. This is why adversity makes some and BREAKS others. At 31 years of age, I have experienced more than most people in their 30's. My bank account has been in the negative more times than I can count. I've failed, loved, lost, and pretty much everything in-between. I've also won, bounced back, fought, and experienced some of the greatest moments that life has to offer. I've witnessed death and also watched the miracle of life. However, there is one life experience that has shaped me far beyond any other – my father's battle with cancer.

It was during this time that I learned how to STRIVE in a world of uncertainty and become stronger during a crisis. Regardless of what occurs in my life, I'm able to handle it due to two principles and guidelines that I learned during this challenging time. These two points are simple, yet, powerful!

THE FIGHT

KNOW YOUR IDENTITY

BELIEVE & EMBRACE UNCERTAINTY

KNOW YOUR IDENTITY

> "But, if you break the moment down into its simplest form, – nothing had changed ..."

It's easy to get lost in life, especially when you're going through something that's painful, unknown, or frightening. For example, when the average person experiences a moment of fear, it can lead to a loss of mental processing and an inability to control one's actions. Let me ask you a question, have you ever been so afraid that you literally freeze in the moment? The point where you attempt to talk, yet, the words won't come out of your mouth. A period where you attempt to run, but your legs feel like you're wearing 100-pound ankle weights. It's a natural reaction; for a moment, we lose our identity. We aren't our normal selves and forget how to do something as basic as speak or walk.

Now, imagine if this happened to you every single day. If at every moment that you experienced something frightening or uncomfortable, you shut down or turned into somebody else. This was how I felt the moment that I found out my father was diagnosed with cancer. I became speechless. My entire body felt like I was wearing one giant body weight. I wasn't "me." I couldn't think for myself. I struggled to drive a vehicle. My entire body and mind turned to mush.

This was a moment of me losing my identity. I couldn't physically nor mentally handle the stress or fear associated with this adverse moment. I felt helpless. I felt crushed. I often questioned God and asked Him, "Why are You doing this to me?" Looking back, I now realize that I didn't know my identity. I didn't know who I was, nor what I was capable of.

It's funny because, we often run away from scary situations since they make us feel uncomfortable. It's the fight or flight mentality. As humans, we naturally fear change; I was scared s***less of the change that was occurring. But if you break the moment down into its simplest form, nothing had changed other than the fact that I received the information. My father was already sick, his body was already fighting this disease. I had no control over the situation. This wasn't some guy on the street trying to pick a fight with my Pops… I couldn't jump in to help him. This was a terrible disease that was eating away his body, and something that had been materializing for years.

So, what was I afraid of? Was I afraid that my father would die? Yes, of course I was, and in that moment, that's where I thought my fear stemmed from. It was a selfish moment. I feared losing someone so close to me, yet, it wasn't until years later that I realized my true fear was receiving the information.

The fear was CREATED BY ME! This disease had planted itself into my father YEARS ago, yet, I never feared it. I never even thought about it because it was unknown. However, as soon as I learned of this information, my body completely shut down. So, I asked myself, "Who are you, and why does knowing this information change your identity?" I couldn't answer it.

Thus, I went on a mission to discover who I really am. I used this time of crisis to find my identity. I decided to explore myself, which may not have been the case if this experience never occurred. Through the persistent efforts of a close friend, I joined a local church and discovered Jesus. I began to understand the positive effect that believing in a power bigger than you and keeping a positive mindset can create.

Time passed, and my father's battle continued. He underwent countless surgeries and periods of recovery; I will talk about this in greater detail later in this book. One day, the doctor said that he was in remission. I can't even begin to describe the joy that I felt in that moment. But… the battle wasn't done. In fact, it was just getting started. A month or so later, we found out that the cancer was back and more aggressive than before. This time, the information hurt badly again, but it didn't cripple me like it did the first time. I never took the time to ask myself why, but, looking back, I was on the journey to finding my identity and I had taken steps in the right direction.

Quick disclaimer: I'm not saying that you should never get sad or that you should quit mourning. That's a part of life that never goes

away. We all cry, and I believe grieving is an important part of life because it helps us heal. What I am
saying is that we can't let it cripple
us. We can't use a difficult time
as an EXCUSE to sit back and become helpless! Unfortunately, this is
something that I believe we all do
far too often. We use a difficult life
experience to say, "I didn't do this

> "I think that it's important to be aware of the fact that your identity isn't just one thing."

because..." Or, "I was on track to graduate, but..." Or, "I could have,
but... happened."

I could have stopped everything as soon as I learned about the
information regarding my father's illness. I had an easy excuse, "I was
in law school, but then, I decided to move home to help take care of
my father." That could have been my escape and an excuse that many
people would "understand." WRONG! I would have hurt so many
people by doing that... my father included. My father was a proud
man; he hated it when people did things for him. He liked to do everything himself and wanted life to appear as normal as possible for
me and my family. Therefore, coming home to help him would have
sped up his death. He would have felt an emotional pain in "holding
me back," since all he ever wanted was to see his children succeed.

Additionally, I would have crushed myself. I'm sure that I could
have thought of countless other excuses to not finish what I started.
I could have lived one giant lie. Instead, I stayed in school, found
solutions instead of excuses, and found my identity during this time.
I discovered my strengths, weaknesses, what makes me tick, my mo-
tivators, and things that I tend to use as an excuse.

I think that it's important to be aware of the fact that your identity isn't just one thing. For example, my identity isn't being a sports
agent. Being a sports agent is what I do, but it's not who I am. Similar
to a fingerprint, each of us have our own identities and they are all extremely unique. Sure, we all share common traits, but it's the unique

combination of those traits that make all of us who we are. And once we discover who we are, we become secure and very powerful.

Discovering my identity led me to find strength that I never knew existed, let alone possessed. It also enabled me to help others, and enjoy life experiences that I would have never dreamed of. I don't know when or if I would have ever discovered my identity if this difficult period in my life never occurred, but looking back, I'm blessed to have gone through a dark, difficult, and idle time because it enabled me to find myself; the experience has also given me the ability to help many others do the same.

So, how can you find your identity during a difficult time? First, you have to be realistic with yourself. I know that it sounds simple, but many of us don't practice this. Staying positive and optimistic makes your entire body feel better, but simultaneously, you have to be very realistic with yourself and learn to not sugarcoat the harshest realities of the world. There have been times in my life where I didn't want to accept reality; where I wanted to believe that I passed an exam, even when I saw the failing grade. "The teacher doesn't know what he/she is talking about." Or, "The referee said that I lost the fight, when I believed that I won." Yes, I was delusional and most of us are. It happens.

Additionally, many of our parents have been subconsciously teaching us these false realities since we were toddlers. Have you ever heard the expression, "My child can do no harm"? Every parent believes that their kid is the best at whatever it is he or she is doing. Let's be honest, this isn't real. I've heard some kids who clearly don't possess a musical bone in their body play the trombone or piano. Yet, this is what we are taught. We have become accustomed to hearing "good job," even when we don't do something correctly or perform at a high level because we're afraid to hurt our feelings.

Unfortunately, this doesn't prepare us for real life. Life can be cruel! There are winners and losers. There is death and life. There are people who get hired and people who get fired. And, usually, life doesn't offer participation trophies. Don't get me wrong, I understand encouragement and believe it's important to motivate those around you. At the same time, not everything is for everyone. So, be realistic with yourself and those around you. The faster we can be honest with ourselves, the faster we can start to find our true identity.

> "What do you go to bed dreaming about? What do you wake up in the morning and to pray about?"

So, where can you start? Here are five action items to help you become realistic with yourself and succeed during this process:

1. **Take Ownership.** Admit that you're wrong or that you've messed up. Own your mistakes. Learn to become comfortable with telling yourself the truth about the situation. And remember, not everything is for you!

2. **Reflect.** Retrace your steps to see what you can do differently. If you failed, use this process to discover why you failed. For example, if you did not pass your exam, was it due to you not studying enough or was it due to how you prepared? What can you do differently? This step is extremely important! This is where your honesty truly kicks in. You have to look yourself in the mirror and admit why you failed, then take that reasoning and begin to correct it.

3. **Prepare.** Use the tools and lessons that you discover during your reflection period to create a better plan for your future preparations. Start to map out how your day, week, month, and year is going to look. What is your roadmap for success? Use the tools you discovered from steps 1 and 2 to create a better plan for yourself… an excuse-free plan!

4. **Learn.** Learn from all wins and losses. It's okay to accept the fact that you will lose far more than you will win in life. But how will you handle defeat? Learn to treat each loss as an important lesson and use that information to succeed.

5. **Conquer.** Eliminate all excuses for failure and seize the opportunity in front of you! You're ready to take over!

Second, you have to find out what it is that makes you tick. What do you go to bed dreaming about? What do you wake up in the morning to pray about? These are the things that typically matter the most to you, so, why not spend more time working toward them? I'm a firm believer in loving whatever it is that you do in life. For me, I discovered that my passion is to help others. This is the main reason that I initially applied to law school – I wanted to become a criminal defense attorney to help my friends and other individuals who I believed were wrongfully imprisoned due to the corrupt justice system. Even though my career path has changed and has led me to become a sports agent, my passion has remained the same. I care about my clients. I form strong personal relationships with them and help them succeed in life. And I am able to use this platform to help countless individuals around the world.

So, what's that passion in your life? What do you not only enjoy, but actually feel a strong connection to? I don't believe it's something you'll discover overnight. It took me years to realize my passion, despite that it has always been there. Maybe that's the same for you. Actually, I'm sure that's the same for you. Your passion, your calling, the thing that you love… well, it's already inside of you. It's up to you to take the time to recognize and discover what that "thing" is and start your new journey in life.

Finally, you have to dedicate the proper time and energy toward your discovery conquest. Like anything else in life, discovering your identity is a process. It requires patience, meaningful conversations, quiet moments, prayer, and time. Make sure that you allow yourself to spend the proper time as you perform a deep dive on YOU! I'm not saying that you need to light up a bunch of candles, lock yourself in a dark room, and meditate. Shoot! For some of you, that may actually work, but we're all different.

I found my time and peace in many different places. Sometimes,

I'd get into my car and just drive. No music, no cellphone; just me and the road. This was my alone time and a break from all distractions. I learned a lot about myself during these drives and I would have meaningful, open, and honest conversations with Jesus about life. I'd ask Him questions and would express my worries, fears, and doubts. There were times where I would admit to something that prior to the drive, I had no idea I even felt or feared. This time alone really helped me discover myself and I believe that it will help you unlock new chapters in your life as well.

BELIEVE & EMBRACE UNCERTAINTY

We all believe in something different. Some of you may believe in a God. Or maybe you believe that life started through science. Or maybe you believe that life is a false reality and that we are merely in an elongated dream. Regardless, we all believe in something. We form our own version of reality and become focused on that perception of it.

I'm going to keep it very simple. We all live and we all die, no matter what it is that you believe in. Yet, while we are on this earth, I think it's important that you believe in something, regardless of whatever or whoever that something is. For me, this "something" is Jesus Christ. He has helped me navigate through some of the most challenging times that life has thrown my way. *Quick disclaimer:* Please understand that I'm not here to persuade to believe that Jesus is the only answer for you; however, for me, He is.

Before I started my faith journey, I was lost, misguided, and felt like I could control every situation. Yet, when something didn't go my way, I blamed the world around me. It was never my fault. I would question why things didn't go my way, but I never had an answer. I was a lost human merely searching for a solution.

Now, things are different. I understand that I don't and won't always have the answer. I've accepted that MOST things are out of my control and I trust that Jesus will help guide me through whatever situation that I'm in. This has been extremely crucial during the pandemic our world has been facing since 2020. For the first time, at least since I have been alive, the entire world has stopped and nobody has an answer as to what's next.

It's still crazy to think about. One minute, I'm at the Super Bowl in Miami, FL then in Indianapolis, IN for the NFL Combine, then suddenly, all sports stop. My clients were calling me daily to ask questions that I simply didn't have an answer to. "What will happen to the season?" "What's going to happen with the NFL Draft?" "Will I get to play this year?" "Will my team still pay me if the season doesn't happen?" This was all brand-new. It wasn't something that I learned in law school, neither did I learn it in my training as an NFL agent.

I called NFL general managers, scouts, coaches, and media personnel, attempting to secure any information that I could. The NFL Players Association held weekly calls, yet, nothing ever seemed to get answered in those calls other than the "we're working on it" and "this is a novel and emerging virus" answers. Nobody had a clear-cut answer. Our world of uncertainty became that much more uncertain.

I conveyed the same message over and over again to my clients, "We have to just control what we can control. Right now, everything pertaining to the season and the NFL Draft is out of our control. Trust in God's plan and just be ready to go." That was all that we could do, and that is what got us through the pandemic – trusting in God's plan and knowing that He had something special lined up for us.

Our agency got creative and hosted individual workouts for our clients. We flew a retired scout into Fort Lauderdale so that he could come conduct a "mock pro day" workout for one of our clients. A pro day is a workout similar to the NFL Combine that's typically held at the athlete's University, where an athlete showcases his physical and mental abilities through a series of workouts.

It's a very important part of the NFL Draft process because it gives teams a chance to watch the athlete perform drills and conduct interviews with their organization. However, in 2020, COVID forced all colleges to shut down and cancel their Pro Days. NFL teams shut down travel for all of their scouts. Thus, nobody was able to come time the athletes during their 40-yard dash or other drills, watch their positional workouts, or conduct any in-person interviews prior to the NFL Draft. All Pro Days came to an abrupt halt!

I felt terrible and helpless for our clients. They spent January, February, and March training non-stop for this opportunity; an opportunity to showcase their speed, agility, and get face-to-face interviews with their new potential employers. They had sacrificed time away from their friends, family, and anything else they could have been doing to train for this day. All of the blood, sweat, tears, and time to get to this point, and suddenly, it's cancelled. No warning. No direction as to what is next.

We had to get creative. This is why we decided to fly in a retired scout to conduct a workout for our clients. The scout was well-known in NFL circles, has credibility attached to his name, and he could run the Pro Day just like one that would have been held at the school. Our agency also hired a film crew to video the entire workout and interviews, so that we could send it to every NFL team. Thankfully, we were able to get it done just before the government shut down all parks and fields. Afterwards, every agency in the country attempted to follow suit, after a reporter broke the news on our "mock" pro day.

We weren't going to let this hurdle completely disrupt us. It definitely wasn't going to cripple us. We just controlled what we could control and believed that Jesus would handle the rest.

A lot of people viewed this time of "idleness" as a loss that they simply couldn't bounce back from. Don't get me wrong, there were a lot of losses as a result of this pandemic … lives, jobs, homes, meals, etc. Yet, there was nothing we could do about this pandemic. It was happening and we were going to lose certain things. For me, the bigger question became, "What victories are going to come from this giant hurdle?"

Losses happen to everyone, but let me just give you one piece of advice: GET COMFORTABLE LOSING! Yes, I know you don't want to hear that. We all want to win. Trust me, I'm an extremely competitive person and so, I hate losing. I don't care if you challenge me to a game of checkers, in my mind, I am going to win. But, I had to learn to get comfortable with knowing that losses are going to occur.

I mean, look, if 2020 has taught us anything, it's to be ready for the unknown. We have to be ready and willing to adapt at all times. For those of us who don't adapt, well, we get left behind. It's that simple, and we see it every day. So, how do you thrive in a world of uncertainty?

First, you have to accept the fact that you are going to fail in life. Failure should be a motivator, not a prohibitor. I fail daily in my job. Whether it's failing to sign an athlete that I've been recruiting, getting told 'no' by a company, when trying to secure an endorsement deal, or having an athlete get cut by his respective football team… it happens. But, I use that as fuel and motivation. You will not deny me. I'm coming right back at you with everything that I have. That's why I am able to strive in a world of uncertainty.

After you learn how to accept the reality of failure, you then have to learn how to keep pushing forward. How do you get back up once you're knocked down? I know a lot of people who will just roll over and say, "Well, I tried." I don't know about you, but I don't want to be known as a "trier," I want to be known as someone who accomplishes great things. And to become someone who accomplishes great things, you have to learn how to get back up, or, to use a boxing analogy, you have to learn how to take a punch on the chin and keep fighting back.

For some of you, this will be extremely uncomfortable, hence why I say you need to get comfortable with being uncomfortable. It will feel more natural to just roll over and quit. But you have to fight this temptation and come back stronger! So, how do you become comfortable with this? First, repetition. The more that you practice, the better you will become. As humans, we are creatures of habit, and resort to our habits when we become uncomfortable. Therefore, make bouncing back a new habit for you! Train your mind and body to bounce back; to keep fighting.

One of the other tools that I continue to use is asking myself a simple question, "What's the worst thing that can happen?" Usually, the worst thing that can happen is someone telling you "No," which puts you right back in the same spot as you were before you asked. Therefore, nothing really changed. And, if nothing changed, then what are you afraid of? Are you afraid of a simple two-letter word that puts you right back in the same position you were 30 seconds prior to shooting your shot? What if Kobe Bryant was so afraid of missing a shot that he never took one? Would he still be known as one of the greatest basketball players of all time? Probably not. This is why I believe that there is more harm in not trying than in trying. Many times, doing nothing is worse than doing something and failing at it.

To use a football analogy to better explain this situation, picture a Quarterback who is faced with a 3rd down with 15 yards to go. His team is losing by one touchdown, and he has only 30 seconds remaining in the game. The Quarterback has a few options. Do nothing and take a sack, throw a deep ball, or take a knee and let the game end. If I'm the Quarterback, I'm throwing the deep ball every time, and here is why. Let's look at the numbers. What's the worst that can happen? You throw an interception and the game is over. Yet, every other option is a victory! You either throw a completion for a touchdown, throw an incomplete pass and try again, or you draw a pass interference penalty that advances the ball down the field. So, if you look at the situation in its simplest form, your chances of success are 3-to-1, and I like those odds.

It's the same thing when asking for a raise, a promotion, or taking a leap of faith to apply for that next job. What's the worst that can happen? You get told "No," and that is the only negative outcome. Yet, you can get the position, get the raise, or open a door to a completely different career path! Why not take the chance?

If you break this down to its simplest form, then I think you can see that there is nothing to be afraid of. So, what better time than now to go after that new job? Go ahead and ask that girl or boy to go on a date with you. Take a chance on something that you have always wanted to do! It's okay to be nervous, but, remember, the worst thing that can happen is being told "no." And if that happens, nothing has changed other than the fact that you are now taking steps forward toward self-growth.

I speak to this because I have lived it. I took a chance, and it's been one of the best things to ever happen to me. I was told "no" hundreds - if not thousands - of times, yet, I kept fighting. I kept clawing. And now, I am running a sports agency as its' Vice President of Football; the same sports agency that initially denied me. I could have not asked, or just accepted the initial "no," but instead, I went for it. I bet on myself and I like those odds every damn time!

So, if you're struggling with uncertainty or the fear of failure, just take a second and ask yourself, "What is the worst thing that can happen?" If the answer to that question is being told "no," then just go for it. Take that chance and watch how something positive comes from it. Embrace this world of uncertainty and start to strive in it!

TIME

In life, we often attempt to control powers that are out of our control. For instance, we tend to dwell on the past and try to control time through the mismanagement of it. TIME, however, is one element that we have no control over. We can't rewind time, slow it down, or pause it no matter how much we wish that we could. Thus, it's important to remember that we can't travel back in time to recreate or mold our past, but we do have the ability to determine and create our future.

I'm not saying that we should forget our past by any means, since our past has molded us into the people we are today. But I do believe that it's important to not dwell on mistakes from our past because we have the power and ability to make our future into anything that we can imagine, or even things that we could never have imagined. This belief, combined with the finding of Jesus Christ has helped me through some extremely difficult times. There's one thing to remember – Jesus can't help those who don't want to help themselves. We must be willing to change our ways, realize our mistakes, and sacrifice for the future that we strive to achieve. From this point forward, excuses are a thing of the past; something that we don't dwell on.

Now, ask yourself, how do you utilize your time?

Think about your future.

Increase your chances of success.

Make your own path… don't wait for one to be created.

Embark on your journey with Christ. You're never alone!

2. Growing Up

I GREW UP in a small steel mill town in Western Pennsylvania called Stockdale, which is located about 35 miles south of Pittsburgh. Every day, I would see the smoke stacks rising into the murky sky from the giant pipes at the local steel mill, which I believed to be the production of clouds as a kid. Looking back, these chemicals couldn't have been too healthy to breathe in. The trains roared past my house, shaking my bed as I drifted off into my dreams; the dreams of someday leaving this small town and becoming something much greater. I just didn't know what that image would look like.

My town didn't have a ton of things to do to keep us busy. In fact, we didn't have much at all. We had a park, an old baseball field that wasn't taken care of, and a pizza shop. My friends and I had to get creative to have fun and, looking back, we did a decent job of that. Our Park had a basketball court, but only one had a net at all times. The other was several feet shorter and never had a net. Yet, we went out there and played every single day – rain or shine.

The Park was the place where every kid in the town gathered. It's where we had the most epic basketball games, learned how to swing on the swing-set, settled disputes at (fight), but more importantly, a place where we could all gather as kids and have fun being outdoors. None of us had cellphones. Most of us didn't own a video game console. Social media didn't exist. It was just us, our bicycles, gallon jugs of Turner's iced tea, and the park.

Life was simple. It was stress-free. We were just a bunch of kids looking to have fun. I remember this one time when we all bought paint ball guns from Walmart (which was about a 25-minute drive away) and cut a hole in the fence near the steel mill.

There were these abandoned buildings, old train cars, and rusted cranes that sat in a lot that was adjacent to the mill. This became our war zone! If you're envisioning this scene in your head, yes, it sounds like Call of Duty. We hid in the abandoned train cars and broke out the old windows in the buildings so that we could take cover and shoot someone on the other team as they came running by. One of our friends even climbed to the top of one of the cranes to shoot down on the other kids. Looking back, maybe this wasn't the greatest idea in the world, but as kids, we had a blast! It kept us out of trouble (other than the major trespassing issue here). But we weren't doing drugs or anything terribly wrong. We were active and just having fun as kids. This was just one example of the many creative ideas that we came up with to stay busy.

That was our town, and although it was small, and we didn't have much, we made the most of it. Honestly, we didn't know anything else. Most of us never even ventured into Pittsburgh (the "City"), so, Stockdale was all that we knew. It was your traditional small-town atmosphere where everyone in the town knew each other by first and last name, and many families had lived there for generations. For example, my mother and my best friend's mother were best friends in high school. It was only natural for me and Nick to become best friends; our friendship started the day I was born. I can't lie, sometimes, I do miss those simple days. The days at the park with no cellphone, no vehicle, no video games... just me, my friends, my Turner's Iced Tea, and the park.

HOME LIFE

I was blessed enough to grow up with both of my parents. I lived with my mother (Lori), father (Sam), and younger sister (Mara). We were close, like most Italian families, and spent every minute possible together. My mother worked as a dental assistant and my father worked as a shipper in a factory that made cardboard boxes. He worked the midnight shift for the most of my life, leaving the house each night around 10:00pm and returning around 7:00 in the morning. He also had a second job – painting houses and offices where he spent weekends and some weekdays working to generate additional income for our family.

My grandparents, on my mother's side of the family, lived directly across the railroad tracks from our house, which was only a five-minute walk. My grandfather was a steel mill worker and my grandmother a stay-at-home baker, who made some of the best cookies you can imagine. I used to love spending time at my grandparents' house because there was always a lot of food and they had a video game system set up for the grandchildren to play with. My parents never really had food or snacks at our house. To be honest, I only remember us having iced tea, the little thin Totino's pizzas, and Steak-Umms in our fridge/freezer. That was pretty much it. My mother worked a lot, so she very rarely had time to cook for us, and if she did, it was usually Mac and Cheese or spaghetti. She worked tirelessly to provide us with a better future, which was a major sacrifice on her end and led us to became regulars at McDonalds.

My Uncle Chuck (Lori's brother) still lived with my grandparents as he attended college. My Aunt Cathy (Lori's sister) and her husband, my Uncle Bob, lived one block from our house on our side of the railroad tracks. My Uncle Bob also worked in the steel mill. That seemed to be the theme of my family – your traditional hard-working, Pittsburgh, blue collar workers. We had generations of steel mill workers and it seemed to be the natural transition after high school … until the mills started to shut down.

Overall, we were all extremely close growing up, but we never really had a ton of interaction with my father's side of the family. Therefore, to me, family has always meant more than just the people you were born into and share the same blood with. It's those that you spend time with, check on, and truly care about. We spent every holiday at my grandparents' house with our entire family (on my mother's side), eating spaghetti, baked ham, and my personal favorite – meat raviolis from Keystone Bakery. My grandmother was a chain smoker, but for some reason, I always thought that the smell of her cigarette smoke made the food taste better.

Call me weird, but for whatever reason, it tasted amazing. I think that was the secret ingredient for her cookies too, because nobody has been able to make them the same since she passed away. It's like the cigarette smoke added a weird hint of additional flavor that I can still taste when I think of them.

One person who became a large part of my family is my best friend, Nick, who lived two blocks from our house along the railroad tracks. We grew up doing literally everything together and always planned on being neighbors when we both got married. Nick and I were inseparable. We spent every day together, always doing something to stay active. Whether it was going fishing, hunting with our BB guns in his backyard, riding bicycles or dirt bikes, playing sports, or video games at his house, we did it together. Growing up, Nick was the brother that I never had.

Again, life was simple back then and that's the way most people lived in our town. But one of the biggest issues associated with growing up in a small town is avoiding the trap placed by many parents (that most people my age fell into), which is being close-minded. For the most part, the people in my town are extremely close-minded and believe that there's no life outside of our small area ... or at least, they don't care to explore it. Don't get me wrong, it's to no fault of their own because, sometimes, you just don't know what you don't know. But in all of this, my parents were different than most. They always had a bigger vision for me and Mara, which is why they did everything in their power to make sure that we were able to explore other parts of the country and the world. Through shear blessings, hard blue-collared work, and countless sacrifices by my parents, I have seen a lot of places and met a ton of interesting people that helped shape me into the man that I am today. Everything happens for a reason!

As a child, I didn't have a strong relationship with Jesus. My parents wanted to instill the power of Christ and the values associated with attending the Catholic church, but I'll be honest, growing up, I disliked attending "Sunday School" and found myself day-dreaming during our traditional church services. Don't get me wrong, in "Sunday School," I learned stories of the Bible, but I didn't really appreciate the knowledge that I gained. I believed Jesus was the son of God and knew of the power He possessed; however, I didn't have an appreciation for how powerful He truly is. We attended church services almost weekly as a family during my elementary school years, but as Mara and I got older, we slowly began showing up less and less. It's the traditional, "we're too busy right now" excuse that many of us still use today. It's the easy way out and the lazy way of saying, "I just don't feel like going," but it makes us seem like we still "wish" that we could be there. I know what you're thinking, "that's a lame excuse." You're 100% correct. Sometimes, when you're in the moment, you start to actually believe your excuses and lie; this is why your excuses need to stop today!

To be perfectly honest, we were a really busy family on the weekends. I had karate, soccer, and hockey tournaments while my sister competed in soccer, cheerleading, and gymnastics competitions. Most of the time, we were on the road, attending some sort of competition or event. But where there is a will, there is a way, and for anything important in life, we must find a way to MAKE time. Attending service at our physical location or not – we could have made time as a family to pray together. We could have made time to form a bond closer and centered around our God. Yet, we didn't. We were so consumed with our earthly desires that we never dedicated the proper time to talk with or honor our Lord and Savior.

As a result of this, I didn't know much about Jesus, nor did I ever really read the Bible. I knew that Jesus died on the Cross for our sins, but that was pretty much the extent of my knowledge. For most of my childhood (even into my early adulthood), I was ignorant of Jesus' power and didn't understand the true control that He had over my life... if I just surrendered that control over to Him. My father would always say, "Everything happens for a reason, even if we don't know that reason yet. God has a plan for us all. He knows our date of creation and expiration." This is a saying that I have adopted and use nearly every day of my life.

To me, my father's saying is deeper than simply words that I utter. It's a lesson centered around patience and trust. We must learn to trust Him with all things, especially those out of our control, and have the patience to see His plan through. Remember, God has a unique plan for your life! Your journey will be different from everyone else's, but that's what makes it YOURS! Embrace the uniqueness of your life. Welcome the hurdles and challenges, and turn over all control to Jesus, then watch how He shapes your life into more than you can imagine!

3. My First Love

WHEN I WAS three years old, I wanted to be like my Uncle Chuck, so, my parents enrolled me into Tae Kwon Do, a form of martial arts that focuses predominantly on kicking. My uncle is a fifth-degree black belt and taught classes at a local karate school called BCAC Academy of Tae Kwon Do. I still remember my first experience there. All of the students were screaming with each strike as Master Forte led the class, "One, AYA! Two, AYA!"

It seemed like something out of a movie. But at my young age, I didn't like the noise, so I asked my parents to take me home. That could have been the end of my fighting career; however, deep down, there was something inside of me that wouldn't let me give up. A couple of months later, I asked my parents to take me back to Master Forte's class with my uncle, and I soon fell in love with the sport; not to mention, I was pretty good at it. I quickly rose in rank within the gym and started to attend the more advanced classes in the evenings in addition to the classes that I was taking in the afternoon. Essentially, I became a "gym rat" and earned my Black Belt by the age of 9, which is the highest honor in martial arts. I was the youngest member in the history of my gym to earn this honor, but it didn't come without hard work, dedication, and sacrifice.

I worked 7 days a week, 365 days a year to capture my goal. I would wake up an hour and a half before I had to walk to my bus stop so I could do 1,000 sit-ups before I had to head to school and would do another 1,000 sit-ups prior to going to sleep. This was something that I picked up from Ken Shamrock, a former UFC fighter and WWE Superstar. My uncle told me that Ken was doing 2,000 sit-ups a day, which allowed him to withstand punches and kicks to his abdomen without getting the wind knocked out of him. I still don't know whether or not this was true, but it definitely helped me. I was shredded as a little kid!

I competed in tournaments across most of the east coast in the United States. I fought in and won the Arnold Schwarzenegger Classic in Ohio. I became a seven-time Pennsylvania State Champion, and added a National Championship to my resume all before the age of twelve. I was an eleven-year-old kid fighting and competing against seventeen-year-old high school students... and winning! At the time, it was a blast. I enjoyed the strategy and art associated with fighting. I would train, come in with a game plan, and execute the plan to the best of my abilities. There was nothing barbaric about it; if anything, it felt therapeutic to me. It was beautiful to watch. I learned some of my most important life lessons through martial arts. I credit Tae Kwon Do for playing a huge role in where I'm at today.

Tae Kwon Do taught me that with hard work and discipline, I could accomplish anything that I set my mind to. It provided me with a solid foundation that I've carried throughout my life. It's my belief that having a solid foundation - no matter when that foundation is formed - is crucial to living a successful life. You have to know what you believe in, what your morals are, develop productive habits, and set goals. You don't build a skyscraper without a blueprint, so, why should you build your life without a plan? If you don't have some form of plan or some passion, then you will spend your life walking aimlessly.

One of the most important traits, but probably the most difficult to achieve is, mastering the art of discipline. It's even more difficult to develop discipline in today's youth due to the continual advancement in technology, which makes it hard to stay focused. There are literally distractions everywhere you look, and children have become accustomed to doing everything electronically, which desensitizes them at a young age. Video games, cellphones, and instant messaging make it difficult for our younger generation to witness raw emotion, since physical interaction has become more limited than ever. Thus, despite that technology has enabled us to remain connected at all times, it has simultaneously widened the gap between human interaction.

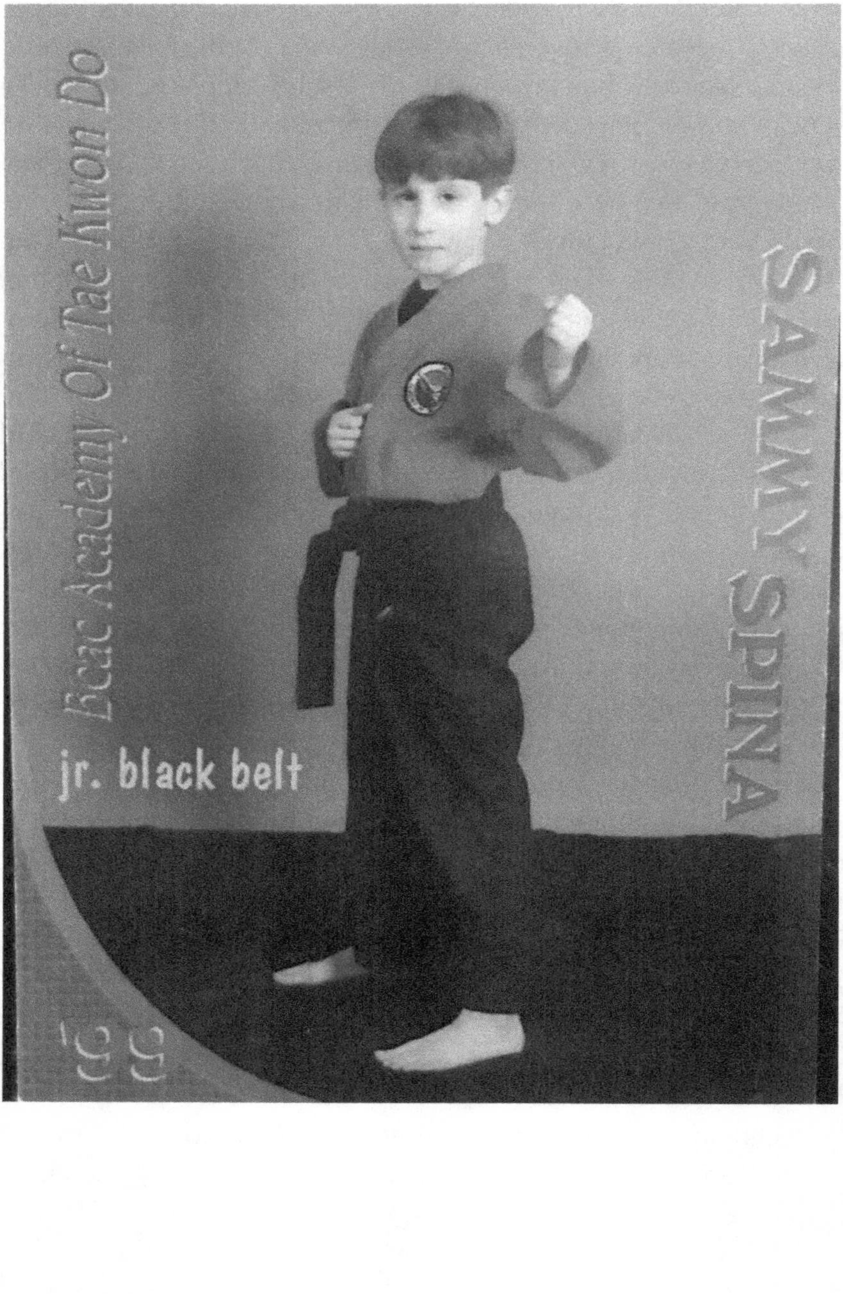
Ecac Academy Of Tae Kwon Do
jr. black belt
SAMMY SPINA

It's become an addiction! I've seen college students spend upwards of twelve hours in one day, playing Call of Duty, essentially wasting an entire day in front of their TV screen. Don't get me wrong, technology can be a great tool if we use it productively, which is why we must learn to use technology in moderation and not let it fully consume our lives nor become a "distractor." As helpful, convenient, and addicting the Internet and video games may be, we need to remain disciplined and focused on obtaining the goals we seek to accomplish.

I get it. It can be tough to put your phone down, and it's difficult to stop yourself from scrolling through social media. I've met tons of people who actually become anxious if they don't have their phone in their hand. It's now easy for me to spot someone who is feeling anxious because when they are in an uncomfortable situation - even meetings - they will start scrolling though social media or old text messages just to make themselves feel slightly at ease. They aren't intentionally being rude or disrespectful, it's just a comfort thing, to suppress their anxiety.

Our society is so used to having everything happen instantly, that hard work and uncomfortable circumstances produce instant anxiety, which triggers most of us to use our cellphone as a form of medicine. I'll admit it, I'm one of those people too. So much so that when I was in law school, I had to download an app that restricted the access to my phone while I was studying for exams. The app allowed me to change the settings in my phone, so that I could only receive and make calls to select people. More importantly, there was a setting that wouldn't let me access social media during a specific time period each day.

This was me being self-aware. I knew that I would become distracted by my phone, so I eliminated that distraction. I made sure that (like it or not) I had to remain disciplined, and focus on my studies. So, I'm not saying you should throw away your phone or quit playing video games, I'm just suggesting for you to start using "distractors" in moderation. Find a balance for your life and do whatever it takes to stick to it.

Discipline yourself to stay focused and dedicate all of your energy toward accomplishing your goals. It's easy to understand what you need to do to accomplish something great, but it's difficult to sacrifice the time and energy necessary toward capturing that greatness. This is the main reason why very few people reach their dream goals without settling for something of lesser value. People tend to fail because they find excuses for their lack of dedication and lack of self-discipline. Just like training for a marathon or a big game, discipline requires preparation and practice. You have to train yourself to remain disciplined!

In Tae Kwon Do, we trained our minds just as much as our bodies. I learned "mind over matter" and how to push myself to limits that I didn't even know existed. Yet, to do this, I had to have a disciplined mind, and to have a disciplined mind, I had to train it. Looking back, it's fascinating how something that many individuals view as a physical sport taught me so many core values and mental lessons that I continue to use today. We learned discipline in all forms, and it started with following instructions. I learned how to put

> Try to use distractors in moderation!

my ego aside and allow for my Sensei to yell at me, teach me, and follow his/her instructions to complete the drills how he/she wanted them done, not what was comfortable for me. I learned about respect and treating people the right way. I learned how to put my emotions aside and remain calm in stressful situations. And I learned that you can do anything that you set your mind to!

One of the earliest accomplishments that I can remember is breaking my first wooden board. Our dojo held demonstrations at local fairs, schools, and events to showcase the talents within BCAC. One of the most exciting things (to me at least) was when the older students used to break boards and cement blocks with their bare hands. I always wanted to try it. Then, when I was about seven years old, my time finally came! I remember staring at the piece of wood, which was held up by two cinder blocks, and thinking "this is it … I'm about to break my hand trying to break this board." My first strike "BOOM!" I smacked my hand on the piece of wood and the board didn't break. My hand started to throb, but the pain was temporary.

Master Forte looked at me and said, "What's wrong? Why did you hesitate and not fully trust yourself to give it your all? You let up because you were afraid of hurting your hand, which caused you to hurt your hand." Let me repeat that, "You were afraid of hurting your hand, which caused you to hurt your hand." In my head, I was thinking, "Of course, I did. It's a 1 ½" thick piece of wood that I'm trying to break with my bare hands." I wasn't utilizing the discipline that Master Forte and our other instructors taught me over the years. I needed to put my emotions aside and trust the process. Instead, I let fear and anxiety cripple me, which ultimately led to my own pain and failure because I was afraid to give it my all. It had nothing to do with my talents or abilities … I had those and I was more than ready. I just didn't trust that I was ready, which caused me to fail. I held back and didn't give it my all.

It was in that moment that I took a deep breath, re-disciplined my mind, and decided to give breaking the board another shot. I did what my uncle and Master Forte told me – envision my fist going straight through the piece of wood. I was taught to aim and strike through the object, picturing the board to be thicker than it actually was. The room around me shrunk, all commotion ceased, and all that I could see was the object in front of me. "AYA!" Suddenly, I came back to reality and heard the other students cheering. This time, I did it! My fist went straight through the piece of wood. I was ecstatic and felt like a true badass.

This was my first encounter (that I can remember) of remaining mentally discipline even though my mind wanted me to believe something else. This is something that happens to people all over the world, every single day. The fear of failure or getting hurt (emotionally or physically) cripples them. You end up failing because you're so afraid to fail that you don't allow yourself to give it your all. The crazy part is … YOU'RE READY! You're more than capable of succeeding in that moment, but you just don't believe it. You don't trust it! This is where learned and practiced discipline can make the difference between getting the job or not, and passing the test or failing it. You got this!

Trust me, there were a lot of people who I went to law school with that knew more information than I did, yet, I would outperform a lot of them because I was able to remain calm under the pressure and trust my preparation. If you prepare properly, put in the time, and give it your all, then everything else is out of your control. You have to learn how to embrace the uncertainty and trust yourself! Don't leave any excuses on the table, but learn to accept the fact that failures are going to continue to happen – it's just a part of life. Make yourself a promise that from this moment forward, you will not fail because you are holding back or folding under the pressure. There will be no more excuses in your life! It's time to go for it!

A second trait that successful people possess is mastering the art of sacrifice. I've always believed that nothing worth having in life comes without sacrifice. Even in my younger days, when I didn't understand religion or truly "know" Jesus, I still knew that He made the ultimate sacrifice for you and I. Therefore, if Jesus, our Lord and Savior, is humble and gracious enough to sacrifice for a greater tomorrow for you and I, then we should be honored to sacrifice while we're here on this earth.

To me, sacrifice isn't simply not doing something now so that you can get ahead tomorrow. It's much more than that. It's consistently prioritizing what's important and making sure that you accomplish those important things before doing something for pleasure (no matter how time-consuming or stressful they may be).

Sacrifice is making sure your children have food on the table before you buy something like a necklace; it's finishing that important paper for school instead of playing video games; it's spending quality time with your family instead of hanging out with your friends; it's taking your child to his/her school play instead of watching your favorite

TV show with a glass of wine; it's working three jobs to pay the bills while you attend night school to achieve your master's degree.

And, most importantly, for me, it's making time every single day to have meaningful conversations with Jesus. You have to sacrifice time so that your relationship with Him can grow stronger than ever before.

You may be thinking, "I already know that sacrifice and discipline are both necessary elements to success." True, it sounds pretty basic, but, oftentimes, people merely talk about sacrifice instead of actually sacrificing. If you want something bad enough, then you must learn to discipline yourself, sacrifice your time, and use every ounce of energy in your body to take the proper steps toward capturing that dream.

For example, a lot of people look at my social media pages and believe that I'm "living the dream." The reality is that most people haven't seen the sacrifices that I've made to get where I'm at today, which is still far away from where I will be. I've sacrificed relationships (friendships and romantic), time, partying, holidays, weekends, "off days," sleep, and countless material objects. I've been so broke that I didn't know how I was going to eat dinner, let alone pay my rent. But I wasn't going to let that become an excuse for my failure.

I'll share a quick story to illustrate what I'm talking about. In my line of work as a sports agent, we have to recruit potential clients while they are still in college, with the hope that the athlete will sign with me after he completes his final college football game. To put this into perspective, every agent wants to sign a first-round draft pick, yet, there are only 32 athletes selected in the first round of the NFL draft each year, and there are more than 800 registered athlete agents. Therefore, you have more than 800 agents competing for 32 spots every single year. So, in order to even be considered by the athlete, agents need to form a relationship, spend the time necessary to develop trust, and stay up-to-date on all information concerning the athlete, his family, his school, his team, etc. Therefore, it's an understatement when I say that I spend a lot of time on the road, traveling from city to city.

Back to the story about how one of my first athlete-recruiting trips took sacrificing dinner for a week. I had $30.00 in my bank account at the time, and nothing in my refrigerator. I'd been attempting to get in contact with an athlete that I wanted to represent for months. Finally, a friend of mine found the athlete's contact information and sent it to me. I instantly gave the athlete a call to introduce myself, and asked if he would be willing to meet with me in person in the near future. He said, "I'm free this Saturday if you want to come meet with me." I had a choice to make and needed to get resourceful to execute it. Now, let me paint this picture a little more vividly. This was Thursday night. I was in Miami, FL (still in law school). The athlete attended a school in Pennsylvania, approximately an hour and a half's drive from Pittsburgh. So, I would need to find a flight out of Miami (the next day), get to Pittsburgh, find a vehicle, drive to the meeting, get back to the airport, and fly back to Miami… all on a $30.00 budget.

I decided that I was going to do whatever it took to make the trip happen, so I confirmed a time with the athlete for that Saturday afternoon. I immediately called my cousin, who's a pilot for a major commercial airline company and asked if I could get a "free" family ticket back to Pittsburgh to go see my parents. Thankfully, he came through and got me a ticket for a Friday evening flight. Next, I called my mother and explained the situation to her. I didn't have enough money to rent a vehicle, so I asked if I could borrow her car. She agreed. I was 2 for 2 and hadn't spent a penny out of my $30.00.

On Saturday, I woke up and took the one-and-a-half-hour drive to meet with the athlete. The meeting went well; he was a really smart young man. I found out that he taught himself Mandarin (one of the most difficult languages to learn) and had become fluent in the language. I learned a lot about him outside of football; something I believe to be very important. The athlete, however, had no idea what I went through to make the meeting work. I wasn't looking for sympathy, I just wanted to do whatever I had to do to make it to that meeting. I was there to work!

Ultimately, he decided to sign with a different agent, but I took the loss as a lesson. There's always a lesson to learn after suffering a defeat. The lesson that I learned was that no matter how hard you try, some things just don't work out, and that's okay. The important thing is that you try! I would have been extremely upset with myself if I didn't at least try, because if I didn't go to the meeting, I would've had a 0% chance of signing the athlete.

A boxing analogy for this situation is that there is always "a puncher's chance." If you aren't out there, throwing punches, then you won't have a chance to win. So, even though I wasn't happy with the result, I am happy that I went.

The point that I'm trying to make here is that it takes sacrifice to achieve desirable results. Even though this one instance didn't turn out the way that I had hoped, I still came closer than a lot of other agents who weren't willing to sacrifice. To be honest, this is the only reason why I'm at where I am today. I'm willing to go above and beyond to dedicate myself and sacrifice things to achieve my goals. I'd be lying if I said it gets easier because it doesn't; however, it becomes more routine, and the victories feel amazing.

This is why it is important to find your "why" in life; your motivating factor; the thing that you can't stop thinking about, and go dedicate yourself to that. Make the proper sacrifices with your time, finances and energy, and then watch how magical the results will be! You won't be disappointed.

CONTINUE TO CHALLENGE YOURSELF

At the age of twelve, I began to fade away from my once beloved sport of martial arts. I had already won a state and national championship, so I wanted to challenge myself in a new realm since I wasn't able to advance in rank until my sixteenth birthday, which was when I could earn my "first degree" black belt. That was still four years away, so I began to focus on other sports such as soccer and hockey. I knew that it would take a lot of work to become elite in either sport, therefore, once again, I became obsessed with trying to become the best at both sports.

One trait that I possess (for good or bad) is the obsession of not wanting to fail or be bad at something. If I find something that I enjoy or want to improve at, then I become obsessed with that particular objective. It's almost as if the world around me shuts down and my sole focus becomes finding ways to obtain that objective. It's the only thing that I think about every free second that I have. I'll day-dream about the sport or goal over and over again, picturing the end result that I wish to achieve. I literally envision success in my mind! Then I spend every free moment of my time practicing, learning, and work-ing toward that objective. I dedicate the time necessary to learn and improve!

Thus, when I started to develop a passion for soccer and hockey, I didn't just dip my feet into the water, so to speak. I dove in head first and joined dek, ice, and roller hockey teams, which gave me the opportunity to play the sport all year round. I was also on a travel soccer club and played for a CUP (advanced travel league) soccer team. Needless to say, I was extremely busy in my early teens. While most kids my age were watching TV shows or playing video games, I was always at practice, a game, or spending time with my family. Hockey, however, is unlike any other team sport I've ever played. I had early morning practices (as a kid) because getting time on the ice was cheaper at 5:00am than in the afternoon. We also had to travel more frequently to tournaments and games, since you played mul-tiple games a week, usually at different rinks. Traveling to these tour-naments were some of the most memorable experiences of my life.

One of the funniest stories that my father always shared with my friends occurred on a hockey trip to Boston, MA. While we were in our team hotel, my teammates and I decided that we wanted to ex-plore the swimming pool area, which also had a sauna. After we got out of the water, we all entered the sauna to dry off and brought a plastic toy boat in with us. I told my teammates, "Watch this! I'm go-ing to make a steamboat," and placed the toy boat onto the hot coals in the sauna. The next thing I knew, a thick white cloud of smoke began pouring out of the small room and into the pool area.

After seeing the smoke, a guest at the hotel pulled the fire alarm, which caused the entire hotel to evacuate. We ran so fast out of the pool area and into the front parking lot area of the hotel, that I could have sworn I ran a 4.2 second 40-yard dash. When I found my parents outside, my father saw me laughing and immediately assumed that I had something to do with this disruption. He was right. I told him what I had done, so he ran back into the hotel, found the sauna and retrieved the toy boat before the fire trucks arrived so that we wouldn't get into any trouble. As I think back and picture this in my mind, it's funny to think about my father standing outside of the hotel with the melted toy boat in his pocket as the fire trucks arrived. But wait, it gets better ….

We watched an entire wedding party exit the hotel out of nowhere. Apparently, a wedding ceremony was going on inside the hotel that morning, so the bride, in her big white dress, had to be carried out of the hotel, down the stairs, and into the parking lot. We created quite the scene in Boston. If you were a part of the wedding that day, I'm sorry for the unfortunate circumstances. I hope the rest of your day went smoothly.

As I got older, hockey started to fade out. I traveled to Canada for tournaments; our team won the NHL Breakout roller hockey tournament two years in a row; I was one of the leading scorers in each of my last three seasons, and I started to develop interests outside of the game. For whatever reason, I couldn't seem to satisfy myself. I always searched for a new challenge and never wanted to settle or become comfortable. This is something that I hope more people will do after finishing this book because, in life, it's easy to get comfortable. Too many of us become satisfied with our progress, start to create lower goals, and tend to blame the culture around us for our lack of motivation. I often hear, "I can't make it out of my neighborhood, no one has," "No one in my family ever went to college," "I'm just not smart enough."

These negative phrases should be erased from your vocabulary;

someone else's past doesn't shape YOUR future. You hold the keys to unlock whatever doors you desire in life, and the only barrier blocking you from the goals you wish to fulfill are the excuses that you create to make yourself feel comfortable with the fact that you stopped pursuing them. Excuses tend to pile up and create a treadmill effect. You say that you want to sacrifice to accomplish your goals, yet, you make excuses as to why you aren't sacrificing. Thus, you're seemingly stuck in the same spot for years, even though you possess a false belief that you're actually moving forward. It's similar to a treadmill, in that, yes, you're moving, but you're moving in the same place. You haven't left the spot you were in, even though you've used up a lot of energy. It's time for you to set the excuses aside, jump off the treadmill, and start taking real steps toward your life goals!

4. Starting to Lose Myself

FOR SOME UNSOLICITED reason, I really started to lose myself in middle school. I began to distance myself from my best friend Nick, and hung out with kids that I probably shouldn't have been hanging out with. I started down a road that I didn't enjoy, but "somehow," I was eventually able to find my path again. To be blunt, I became kind of an asshole. I took a break from both soccer and hockey, but still remained extremely active. I joined the school's football team as well as a youth league team, the school's wrestling team, and the school's track and field team. I was also named class president, was dating the captain of our middle school cheerleading team, and joined almost every organization our school had to offer.

I instantly fell in love with football, even though I was always undersized to play. I didn't expect to have much playing time in my first year on the team, however, one of the benefits of attending a small school was that there wasn't a lot of talent to choose from. So, I came up with a plan on how I was going to fast-track my way into becoming a starter. The coach had me playing defense, so I dedicated my time to learn the plays that the offense ran in practice, ultimately memorizing everything that the offense was going to do, which allowed it to look like I could really read the play and jump the routes that the wide receivers were running in practice. It seemed like I was getting multiple interceptions in every practice, which led me to become the team's starting safety, prior to our first game. That same season, I earned some time at the running back position and became one of our kickoff returners. I have two quick stories that I'll remember for the rest of my life.

First, I always enjoyed returning kickoffs since it felt like a mind game where you had to travel through a maze of people, find the openings, and avoid being tackled for as long as possible. I worked hard in practice, and consistently asked my coach to give me the opportunity to return a kickoff in a game. That time eventually came! It was an evening game at our home stadium. Our middle school team played in the same stadium as our high school team; therefore, the older kids were in the stands, watching us. I stood near our 10-yard line thinking, "This is finally it! I get to show everyone what I can do." Now, before I finish the story, I want to clarify one thing. I had never practiced returning a kickoff at night, under the lights, in a live setting. Regardless, no excuses!

Fast forward – the ball was kicked and I could remotely hear the noise of our school band in the background as the ball floated into the dark sky. Suddenly, I lost the ball while it was in the air and couldn't find it in the bright stadium lights. SMACK! The ball hit me straight in my facemask and landed on the ground. Luckily, my teammate was standing in front of me and was able to grab the ball from the ground before the other team picked it up. I was beyond embarrassed and also disappointed because, I let the lights distract me. I thought and believed that I was ready for this moment, but, evidently, I wasn't. Or maybe I was, and just made a mistake. Either way, I "fumbled" the opportunity.

My second story involves me playing running back. I was extremely small in middle school. I mean, so small that my parents took me to a doctor because they were worried that I hadn't hit my growth spurt yet and thought something could be wrong with me. The doctor wanted to put me on a form of steroid to help me gain weight, but we ultimately decided against doing that. In my 8th grade year, I stood approximately 5'3" and weighed in at a whopping 75 pounds, which I remember, only because I wrestled at 75 pounds, and that was the lightest on my team.

My coaches used to call me "Mighty Mouse" because I never backed down from anyone, even when we would play a game called

"King of the Mat," where one person would start in the middle of the mat and would wrestle for a period of time against everyone on the team, regardless of their weight class. I used to give it my all, even when I was going up against the biggest or heaviest person on the team, because I always believed that I could win.

Back to the story. We were playing a local school, Trinity Middle School, who had two linebackers that weighed over 185 pounds each. My coach called a play that we ran earlier in the season, where our Quarterback handed me the ball; I hid behind the blocker directly in front of me, and took off into the open field after I reached the secondary. The last time we ran this play, the opposing team didn't even know I had the ball until I was 35 yards down field because they simply couldn't see me. Yet, this time, it ended much differently. "HUT, HUT." Our center snapped the ball to our Quarterback, my lead blocker ran through the gap in-between our offensive linemen, and I followed … heading straight toward those two linebackers. Now, one thing to know about young Sammy is that I was always confident. Shoot, I still am today. Needless to say, despite my size, I had the mindset that I was going to run right through those linebackers and anyone else who got in front of me.

So, I took the handoff and ran full speed at those two linebackers, then "BOOM!" The next thing I knew, I was lying on the ground and didn't know what happened. My lead blocker turned to block someone else and those two linebackers hit me simultaneously. It was like hitting a brick wall! I went from running full-speed, to an instant stop, and found myself lying flat on my ass, with the wind knocked out of me, and my mouthpiece laying on the ground beside me because it shot out of my mouth from the impact. We ended up losing that game pretty badly, and the coach decided not to run me up the middle for the remainder of that game.

I tell these two stories to show you how quickly life can change. In my first story, when the football was in the air, I had two goals: (1) catch the ball and (2) score a touchdown. But for a split second, I lost the ball in the lights, which caused it to smack me in the face. In life, you will make goals that you hope to ultimately achieve, but if you let your mind drift elsewhere, you can lose sight of those goals and fall victim to the wrong path, just like I lost sight of the football. It only took a split second for me to go from hoping to achieve my goals, to having them literally smack me in the face!

> "Life is short, and a constant gamble, so, you want to make sure that the odds are stacked in your favor."

The same happens in life all of the time. You can have everything you worked so hard to obtain be taken away in the blink of an eye. The scary part is that it really doesn't take much. All it takes is being in the wrong place at the wrong time, and/or doing something that you know you shouldn't be doing, such as: trying that drug "one time," stealing that "one" item, driving when you had "one" drink more than you know you should have had, or being distracted by your phone while driving. This can also occur in a less extreme manner, such as watching TV instead of working on a side-project that will ultimately lead you toward your goal of financial freedom. If you waste time and lose focus, then life will smack you in the face sooner or later. Remember, you need to ask yourself, how do you utilize your time?

It's important to be cognitive of your actions and realize that just because you did something one time and nothing bad happened doesn't mean that it's acceptable behavior to continue into the future. Each time you do that drug, drive your vehicle under the influence, text while driving, or steal that item, your odds of losing everything that you worked so hard to obtain doubles. Life is short, and a constant gamble, so, you want to make sure that the odds are stacked in your favor.

The second story of me running directly into those two large linebackers is a representation of not letting your pride dictate your life. Sometimes, you will need to think outside of the box and run around the wall that's in front of you, instead of running directly into it. Some things in life are indestructible, and many things are out of our control. Therefore, it's important to learn how to deal with those things, which means taking an alternative route to reach your destination in situations where you have a road block.

Back when I was in middle school, I was stubborn, close-minded, and prideful. I only saw things one way, which is why I ran directly into those two linebackers when the coach called the play. Instead, I should have looked at the situation and realized that I wasn't going to run over those two grown boys. But that doesn't mean that I shouldn't have ran the ball. I could've ran to the outside of my linemen instead of between them, which would have allowed me to avoid the linebackers all together. I had an alternate lane that I didn't take because I was blinded by my own ego, my own close-mindedness, and my own trap that led to my unfortunate outcome. Moral of the story – don't run into the wall that's in front of you. Treat the wall as a construction site that is telling you to take an alternate route – a detour. You can still reach your destination, just don't let anything distract you or discourage you as you follow this new path.

THE WRONG CROWD WILL FIND YOU, IF YOU LET IT

Like many teenagers, I began hanging out with the wrong crowd and made a lot of mistakes. The summer of my 8th grade year, I started smoking weed, drinking, and arguing with my parents. The crazy thing is, I still don't know how I even got started. There was no rhyme or reason. Nobody forced me to do anything, and my parents provided me with everything that I needed to survive and be happy. Yet, I still felt some void, emptiness, and curiosity, which led me to explore this world.

The first time I ever smoked weed and drank alcohol occurred in the same night. A few friends and I decided that we were going to create our own "camp site" as a little get-away from all of the adults in our world. We found a patch of woods near our home and spent days cleaning out the area, setting up tents, and building a small fire pit. We would spend the entire day in the woods, working on making this little camp site look presentable. After it was completed, we started spending summer nights up there. The first night there, one of the older kids brought a case of beer with him. It was a brand called "Stoney's," which is a local Pittsburgh company. That was my first time ever drinking alcohol and getting drunk. As the buzz sank in, I began to really enjoy the smell of the marijuana that was being smoked around the fire. I turned to one of my friends and said, "Hey man, let me try that."

That was the start of it. It was my first experience with marijuana, and I enjoyed the feeling that I got from smoking. All of my stress and worries disappeared. I felt numb to everything around me, and life just seemed more fun. I started smoking before school, before going to practice, and would wait to hear my father leave for work (which I knew was 10:00pm every night) to sneak out of our basement door to go smoke before heading to bed. Back then, smoking weed was much more frowned upon than it is today. You were looked at as a "troubled kid" if you were smoking, but I didn't look at it that way. To me, I was just a kid who liked to smoke and relax. I wasn't causing trouble, unlike some of the people that I knew so, in my mind, it could have been worse.

For example, I remember one morning, a couple of my friends and I were waiting for the school bus at the park. There was this wooden pirate ship in the park that had a little slide and enclosed area toward the bottom of the "ship" where we used to hide to skip school, smoke, or even just use it as a bathroom. But on this day, as we entered the "ship," we discovered another kid (who normally didn't catch the bus at our bus stop) hiding in there.

I recognized this kid. He was a few years older than I was, but he was on the school's wrestling team, so we had crossed paths several times. We asked him what he was doing and he asked for us to be quiet, since he wanted to skip school. In the coming days, we found out the truth. Earlier that morning, he killed both of his adoptive parents and was hiding in the ship from the police. It gets crazier! He actually had a hit list for kids at our school that he planned to kill.

Luckily, he didn't make it that far and was arrested and charged with murder before ever stepping foot on our school property. I'm pretty sure that he remains in prison today.

But back to my story. I started hanging out with this group of kids from the camp site, and carried this friendship into my early high school years. I ended up quitting football due to my lack of size and re-joined the school's soccer team. Looking back on it all, that was the correct decision. I was better at soccer than football and was the only guy on our team to start every single game from my freshmen to senior year. Yet, even with the success I was having on the field, I continued to hang out with the wrong group of people off-the-field, which had now expanded into a group of older kids. It's sad looking back at those days and seeing where everyone's at now. I'm pretty sure that I'm the only person out of that group of kids who hasn't spent time in prison or overdosed on some form of drug. It's crazy to realize that most of my "friends" fell into the trap that so many kids from my high school fell into. The world and environment around them sucked them in… and it's easy to let that happen.

I'll never forget one of the first high school parties that I attended. My friend (who had already graduated) called me during my freshman year of high school and asked if I wanted to go to some guy's house, who I'd heard of, but I didn't know him at all. He told me that we had to hang out at this guy's place, since he was just released from jail and was on house arrest so he couldn't leave his property. I remember that night vividly. As we walked into the house, there was broken glass all over the carpet from a shattered coffee table. Apparently, this guy had broken the table minutes before we arrived, during a fight with his girlfriend. He was still standing in the living room, shirtless, sweat running down his face and chest, and his veins bulging from the adrenaline that he still had from the recent argument. His girlfriend was upstairs, screaming down at him, cursing him out for whatever reason they were arguing.

To paint the picture a little more vividly, he was approximately 6 feet tall and weighed around 200 pounds, recently released from jail, no shirt, tattoos covering his chest, and a monitoring device strapped around his ankle. Remember, this was my freshman year of high school; I was still only about 5'4" tall and weighed roughly 85 pounds. I tried to avoid their argument, so I walked over the broken glass and sat on the couch, not saying a word to anyone in the room.

About three minutes later, the guy walked into the room, came over to the couch, stood directly in front of me, and asked, "Who the **** are you? Did I say you could sit on my couch? Stand your little a** up!" Admittedly nervous, I jumped up as if an army general was barking orders at me. While standing there at attention, I looked him in the eyes to act as if I wasn't afraid (even though I was). He was staring back at me, looking serious and pissed. Suddenly, the guy broke out into laughter and handed me a bottle of Jägermeister and said, "I'm just messing with you little homie. Here. Have a sip and let's have some fun."

Even after all of this, for some reason, I stayed at the party and actually became friends with the guy. I started to fall into the trap of hanging out with the wrong crowd, like many of my friends did, which I attribute to my desire of always wanting to help people escape from difficult situations. I believed that I could save people from the mistakes they were making, but I now realize that you cannot save those who do not wish to be saved. In the words of Pastor Rich Wilkerson Jr., "you have to catch a fish before you can clean it," meaning, you have to start something or want help before you can actually receive it. In my case, before I could provide that help, I needed to find people who were open to receiving it. I could have easily fallen face first into the same trap that many of my friends did, and I saw how easily it happened to them.

Shoot, I could be writing this story from my jail cell right now, asking for forgiveness for something that I had regrettably done. But God had a much larger plan for my life. "Somehow" (I still don't remember why or how) I faded away from that crowd of friends and started to turn my life around for the better. A good friend of mine, Tanner Lakey, once told me that there are many names for Jesus, such as "somehow" or "something." I truly believe that this "somehow," was Jesus directing me back to His chosen path.

As my father would always say, "everything happens for a reason," and I believe the reason I took this route was to gain an understanding of what occurs when you fall into this trap. Now, with the first-hand knowledge that I gained, I hope I can help or save others from taking that route and can help you guide your "Savable Other" back to his or her chosen path. If you're scared, nervous, and/or concerned that your child, parent, aunt, uncle, friend, or teammate is heading down the wrong path, please always remember that there is no stronger power than the power of Jesus Christ. We will refer to the person in your life as your "Savable Other," since there is no such thing as a person who is unsavable. With prayer, determination, persistence, and patience, your Savable Other will be able to find his or her path again.

It doesn't matter what event occurred in your life or the life of your Savable Other, you have to learn how to put that aside and focus on the task at hand. Continuing to hold a grudge or remaining angry at the person is the product of selfish thinking. Christ is forgiving, which means that you should be too. Also, please remember that your Savable Other's deterrence is not attributable to "poor parenting" or something that you caused. So, let's not focus on blame here. This isn't the time to feel sorry for yourself because that will distract you from the task that's now in front of you, which is working with Jesus, or whomever your God may be, to help save your Savable Other.

Sometimes, there is no rhyme or reason for why someone steers down the wrong path. Look at me as the prime example. My family was amazing, supportive, and loving, yet, for some reason, I chose to take the wrong path even as I was always guided in the opposite direction. The same may be true for your Savable Other! If everyone around me had given up on me, then I don't know where I would be at, but I'm sure that I wouldn't be where I'm at today.

STARTING TO FIND MY WAY – KIND OF…

College was always extremely important to my parents. They wanted my sister and I to be the first in our family to attend and graduate, regardless of what we studied. Gaining that knowledge was their way of us making it out of Stockdale and Charleroi, Pennsylvania. Neither my mother nor my father went to college, so I became the first person in my family to attend and graduate, followed two years later by my sister. My mother gave birth to me at a young age and started working right after high school in order to make a living for our family. Therefore, applying to schools was a challenging process for me, since we had zero idea as to what was going on.

Additionally, my high school didn't provide us with the best resources to help with the process. I didn't know anything about applying for scholarships (or that they even existed outside of an athletic scholarship) and knew even less about the financial aid process. But after high school, I was accepted to and attended Washington & Jefferson College ("W&J"), a small private, liberal arts school in Washington, Pennsylvania. The school is extremely difficult to get into, but luckily, the school's soccer coach wanted me to join their team. Since W&J is a Division III program, the school was unable to provide me with an athletic scholarship (due to NCAA rules), but the coach set up a meeting with W&J's Dean of Admission to help make this process as smooth as possible.

For "some reason," I've always strived in interviews. I walked into the room, admittedly nervous, yet, confident that it would all work out. I attribute my calm demeanor to my father since he always believed that "everything will work itself out." My mother, on the other hand, has always been a go-getter. She believes in finding an opportunity, seizing it, and attacking it! Luckily, I have a little bit of both of their genes in me, which is a good combination. I'm like a mutt: calm and confident on the outside, but I am very, very persistent and will jump on an opportunity once I set my mind to it. Long story short, I walked out of the interview with the Dean laughing and giving me a tour of my new home for the next four years of my life. This was going to be a new beginning with a new group of friends that would last a lifetime.

A Love Story

Have you ever been in a relationship for the wrong reasons? Maybe the sex is so good that you don't want to risk losing it. Or you have a fear of being alone. Or your parents really want grandchildren, so you stay with your boyfriend or girlfriend, hoping that the relationship gets better. I get it. It's tough because your head and heart are in a direct conflict and you're being pulled in two different directions. It can be confusing, stressful, emotional, and tiring.

This happened to me during my sophomore year of college when I met a girl that attended W&J. At first, it was innocent. We would hang out, go to parties together, and just talk about random things. We had a lot in common, knew a lot of the same people, but we were also polar opposites with a lot of things. I knew that I wanted to be successful in life, no matter what career path I ultimately chose, but she didn't have her priorities in the same order.

Over time, our innocent "hangouts" turned into real feelings. We started dating each other, sleeping together, and doing pretty much everything with one another. It was cool because we went to the same college and also had a lot of similar friends from back in our hometowns. I knew that she had a rocky past, but I thought that it was all behind her. My friends warned me about her, but I was blinded by my feelings. I saw the signs, yet, ignored them. That's the thing with Jesus, He will provide you with directions, signs, and clues, but He will never force you to do something. It's up to us to trust Him and to follow Him.

Over time, I began to discover that she was using and abusing prescription drugs. Years earlier, she was in an extremely violent accident that nearly killed her and that's where the addiction started, but not where it ended. Her addiction to pain pills led her to experiment with other drugs such as cocaine and heroin. I "somehow" didn't fall into the trap of doing drugs despite falling in love. I would hang out with her, smoke a little marijuana, and drink alcohol, but I never experimented with other drugs. "Something" always kept me from falling into that trap. I thought that her being with me would provide her with the opportunity, power, and support necessary to save herself from the world of addiction.

Unfortunately, I wasn't able to save her from this relentless disease. I fought hard, but she was pulled by a much stronger force in the opposite direction. It was a rough and rocky situation, as our relationship slowly came to a halt. We began to have tough conversations about getting serious help, which often led to arguments. This became a major distraction, since we fought on a daily basis and it started to cause arguments between me and my mother. These arguments became extremely tiring due to all of the emotion and energy spent. After about a month of breaking up and getting back together, we finally decided to just end our relationship and go our separate ways.

Months later, she called me when I was on a golf course with some friends, from an out-of-state area code and a number that I didn't recognize. She told me that she finally took the initiative to enroll herself into an out-of-state rehab facility and had been feeling much better since being there.

Admittedly, I was heart-broken after our break up even though I knew that I had given it my all. I pride myself on always going full throttle and not holding anything back, but sometimes, God has other plans for you. I took this experience as a learning opportunity and came to the realization that you can't help someone who isn't open to receiving help. Looking back, maybe I approached the situation wrong since I believed that I could help everyone. I didn't understand that not everyone wants my help and that they have to be ready to make a change before that change can occur! It's amazing how God continually provides lessons on a daily basis, especially when you aren't searching for that lesson.

When we first broke up, I remember asking, "Why does this have to happen to me?" This was selfish thinking, since the real questions should have been, "What is God preparing?" or "What lessons should I take from this experience?" Here, God wanted to show me that no man nor woman is perfect. Additionally, He showed me that just because you

> "Remember, for every failure, there is a victory!"

give it your all doesn't necessarily mean that it will work out perfectly. Life is full of failures, but it's not the failures that bring you down. It's how you approach, accept, and deal with those failures that shape you into the person you are to become. Personally, I believe failures are accelerators, not inhibitors. By accepting your failures, making mistakes, and realizing that most things are out of your control, it enables you to harness the power to seek alternative routes. It molds your mind to think outside of the box instead of shutting down each time a roadblock gets thrust into your path. There are countless opportunities in this world (not just with dating)! Therefore, failing at one thing opens the door a little wider for you to succeed at something different. Remember, for every failure, there is a victory!

Silver Barrel

W&J was located one street behind the local project plan, which was where a lot of crime occurred. The students at our school labeled the locals who lived in the projects and surrounding communities, "townies," since most of the individuals who lived there didn't attend my college. For the sake of this story, I will continue to use the term "townies" to make things easier, since it also provides you with a better description of how our school perceived my friends. I'll never forget the first weekend of my freshman year of college. For those of you who went to college, you probably remember your first weekend on campus as one giant party, your first college hook up, grueling practices, or stressfully studying to get ahead in class. Mine was a little different.

It started out with me wanting to explore the party scene. I was invited to attend a little pre-gaming party at one of the sorority houses, where one of the older girls that I knew lived at, so I called one of my friends to go with me. We met up and left my dorm room to start walking down the street to her place. As we approached "Greek Row" (a two-block radius where all of our school's fraternities and sororities were located), a car with three individuals pulled up behind us. I looked over at the vehicle as the passenger rolled down his window and asked me to come over to his car. He said, "Where da party at tonight?" I told him that I wasn't sure, since it was my first weekend on campus. He looked me in the eyes, raised his shirt to reveal a gun, and stated, "Let me ask you again. Where da party at?"

At this point, I looked behind me to find my friend who was standing next to me seconds earlier, running in the opposite direction. I responded laughingly, "Like I said, I'm not sure because it's my first week here, but you can look around with me if you want." The individual responded with, "Get in the car."

I'm not going to lie, I got a little nervous at this point, but I remained calm because I knew it wasn't my time to die yet. I knew Jesus had larger plans for me, even though my relationship with Him wasn't strong at the time. I understood how dangerous this situation could potentially be and so, I wouldn't recommend anyone reading this to follow my lead by getting into the car. Regardless, I got into the vehicle and while in the car, the group of guys started asking me a bunch of questions like where I was from, etc. Eventually, the passenger who originally pulled the gun on me looked back and said, "Oh shit. My bad bro, I remember you!" I responded with, "Remember me?" He said, "Yeah man. We were in lock up together. Come on, you don't remember me?" I told him that he was confusing me for someone else, but he didn't believe me and kept telling the others in the car that I was in jail with him at one point, which I never was. To clarify, I have never been arrested (knock on wood).

Long story short, I ended up going out and partying with the guys who pulled the gun on me. We became "friends," exchanged phone numbers, and went to a couple of fraternity parties together that night. Finally, one of the fraternity brothers noticed a gun on one of the individuals and kicked them out of the house. The fraternity called the police and I haven't heard from those individuals since that day.

It was an interesting experience to say the least, but it's one I'll never forget. I remember sitting in the back of their car, passing around a large 7-Eleven slushy cup filled with only God knows what as we drove around Washington, Pennsylvania. As I reflect back, there are so many negatives that could have come out of that situation, and the only real "excuse" that I could use was that I was "kidnapped," but how believable would that have been? Especially since I was passing around a drink in the car with the guys, was seen at multiple parties with them, and was now under the influence. Thankfully, "something" kept me alive and out of trouble that night.

This, however, wasn't my only run-in with "townies" during my time at W&J. I actually became friends with a lot of people outside of our school who lived in the area. I went to house parties and bars that "I shouldn't have been going to" – places where I'd walk into the bathroom and see a guy smoking crack by the sink. Sometimes, I can still smell that nasty aroma. It's one of those odors that you can instantly taste on your tongue as soon as it hits your nose. I'm getting a little nauseous just thinking about it. I could still smell it for days after leaving the place, and taste it for longer than that.

I became good friends with a particular group of people, and after gaining their trust, I never had another issue like the one I experienced during my first weekend on campus. I remember going to one party at some house that I'd never been to previously. I went into the kitchen to grab something from the refrigerator, but when I opened the door, I quickly noticed that it didn't contain any food or drinks. This person had pounds and pounds of drugs "hidden" in there. To this day, I still have not seen that many drugs in one place. After seeing the drugs, I quickly thought of the different situations that could've went wrong, yet, I didn't leave. I stayed and hung out with everyone until about 2:00 am, and then went back to campus.

Looking back, with the legal knowledge that I now possess, I realize how blessed I am for never getting into any trouble. I also understand how these experiences have shaped me into the man I am today. Admittedly, I would never want my future child to put himself or herself in those situations, but I do believe that I've gained a lot of knowledge that I can use to help deter future generations of children from falling into that same trap that almost sucked me in. Having this first-hand knowledge provides me with a different relatability factor that not many people have. Now, it's up to me to do good with that.

5. Fighting Again

ONE OF THE reasons why W&J's Admissions office accepted me into school was the soccer coach's desire for me to play on the school's soccer team, which I did during my freshman year. But then, I decided to quit the team during my sophomore year of college. I wanted to get back into the fighting scene and I couldn't do both, so I chose boxing over soccer. I drove back to my hometown every day, which was about a thirty-five-minute drive, where I dedicated all of my free time to the sport. This was a "real boxing gym" where everything about it was tough. Our gym didn't have heat nor an air conditioner, so, in the summer time, it was as hot as you can imagine, and, in the winter, it was freezing. We didn't have any running water and every single piece of gym equipment had duct tape on it. Our boxing ring was 100% homemade with old two-by-fours standing in the corners as "ring posts," rope that we bought from Lowes wrapped in blue and red duct tape as our ring ropes, and an old wrestling mat as our base. This was our boxing ring, where we sparred on a daily basis.

Eventually, I got pretty good; I fought in the Golden Gloves boxing tournament where I finished as a runner-up, and trained with some of the best professional boxers in the world. With boxing, like everything else I had ever done, I possessed a "never give up" mindset. Here's a quick story about my first fight. One week before the fight, I broke my nose in a training session while sparring with one of the professional fighters at our gym. This was an easy excuse to back out of the fight, but I worked my tail off to get ready for this day!

For those of you who don't know anything about boxing, training for a fight is no easy task. It requires a lot of discipline and sacrifice just to make weight, let alone making sure you're in the physical shape necessary to compete. The very next week, I still showed up to the fight and won, but re-broke my nose in the process.

I'll never forget the feeling I had in the ring during my first fight. My roommate, boxing partner, and my brother from another mother - Kory Imbrescia - drove me to the hotel in Pittsburgh where the fight was scheduled to take place. On the way, I asked him to stop at a Subway restaurant where I ordered a footlong Italian BMT and a large Mountain Dew to eat after I weighed in. I know it sounds strange to drink Mountain Dew before a fight (and it is), but my father started me on that tradition at a young age. Mountain Dew was his favorite beverage, so he would buy one for me before each soccer game, karate tournament, or hockey game as a child. The tradition just stuck with me.

When I entered the ring, it was unlike anything I had ever experienced. When you're in there, it's just you and the man standing across from you. There are no more excuses. If you lose, there is no one to blame other than yourself. When I was in the ring, I was so focused on the task at hand that it felt like I could hear a pin drop. It was as if I was wearing noise-cancelling headphones since everything around me seemed silent. To me, there were only two people in the entire hotel – myself and my opponent. It was as if time stopped and nothing else mattered in that moment.

I was focused, and I was ready. After the fight, I remember asking Kory, "Why was it so quiet during my fight?" Kory laughed and said, "Bro, your fight was the loudest of the night." In fact, it was named "Fight of the Night!" After watching the video, I realized that he wasn't lying. People were screaming and I could hear my mother yelling, "Punch him in the face, Sammy! Hit him again!" When I look back at that moment, it's amazing how the Lord can place you in a situation where everything just stops around you; where all of your worries, fears, and anxieties just disappear. For a second, you feel free. You feel in control. That was one of the reasons why I loved fighting. It took me to a place where I felt free.

After the fight, I took a week off from sparring, and then began

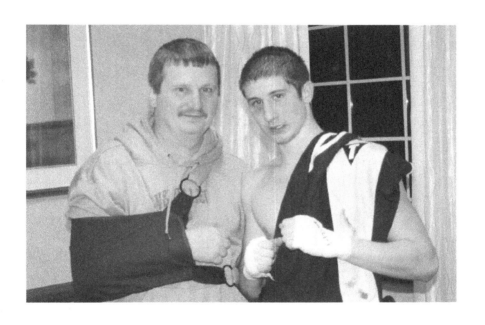

wearing a special headgear to protect my nose from punches during training. Then, two days before my second fight was scheduled to take place, I re-broke my nose for a third time; this time, deviating my septum. Needless to say, I still showed up to my fight. I came in with a plan – I was going to stop the fight in the first round by knocking my opponent out. This way, he wouldn't have the chance to hit me or touch my nose. I even told my Pops on the way to the venue that I planned to win by TKO less than two minutes into the first round. I knew that I was better than this guy, but I needed to make sure that I didn't take any unnecessary punches.

"Ding. Ding." The first round started, and I had my opponent up against the ropes less than 30 seconds into the fight. I landed a flurry of punches and I knew that he didn't have an answer for me. This was it… exactly what I predicted! I'm going to knock him out!

Suddenly, I got careless and dropped one of my hands. I thought the fight was almost over and that the referee was going to jump in to stop it, but I relaxed a moment too early. While my opponent was falling backwards, he threw a single punch that landed directly on my nose. This startled me and led me to go into a protective mode since I instantly saw a stream of blood running down my face. Again, he punched me in my nose. It felt as if my entire nose retracted into my skull and then popped back out. Punch after punch, my nose felt as if it went into my skull, touched my brain, came back out, and fell off. The feeling was surreal, painful, and uncomfortable.

The referee paused the fight since the blood wouldn't stop pouring down my face and asked my corner to stop the bleeding. My trainer put two cotton swabs up my nose, one in each nostril, and added more Vaseline to my face. Yet, the blood kept coming and the cotton went from white to red before we even started throwing punches again. Unfortunately, the referee decided to stop the fight. I lost the fight and bled for more than 45 minutes that night – the longest nosebleed of my life. I continued to box after that; however, I didn't compete in another major sanctioned tournament.

Today, I still have my deviated septum, since I didn't get the surgery to fix it. Sure, it's annoying and makes it difficult to breathe at times, but I don't regret accepting those fights with my broken nose. In fact, I'm happy that I took those fights because I showed myself that I have the heart to fight through ad-

> *"God created humans imperfectly perfect"*

versity, no matter how painful it may be. I'm a fighter and I'm going to keep fighting for as long as I can!

I think this is something that occurs far too often in life. We experience a set-back so we give up on everything that we worked so hard for. We tend to take the "easy way out" instead of facing adversity head on. I've witnessed this a lot in faith journeys. When times get tough, people start to question God instead of leaning in closer to Him. Admittedly, I was that person at one point too. My faith didn't have a strong foundation so it was easy for me to question God.

Now, don't get me wrong, I don't believe Jesus minds you questioning Him. I think He really wants you to speak with Him, even if that starts out by your questioning of Him and His plan. Maybe that's how you start building your faith, by talking with Him in these moments. I challenge you to slowly lean into Him more and more for advice! Then trust His direction! Remember, God created humans imperfectly perfect. We all have our flaws, yet we all possess the ability to keep pushing forward. To keep working when we are tired or don't feel like it. To keep swinging even when we feel like we are losing the fight.

I promise you; you are much closer to victory than you know! Stay positive. Stay consistent. Keep fighting. And become closer with Jesus than you ever have in your life. Your "big break" is right around the corner. Just make sure you don't lose sight of who is guiding your path.

EYE OPENER

During college, "something" opened my eyes and helped me change the way I was approaching my daily life. I stopped smoking marijuana cold turkey. We are now more than 10 years since I stopped and I still don't smoke! I cut back on attending parties. I discovered that I have a strong desire to help others and enjoy fighting for them, which is why I started to think about applying for law school. I figured that becoming a lawyer would enable me to help people (like myself and many of my friends) who had made mistakes in their lives. Everyone makes mistakes, so I wanted to be a part of the process that allowed for second chances. But, like most 20-something-year-olds, I wasn't 100% sure of what I wanted to do.

After college, I took a two-year break from school and worked with my father who had recently quit his job at the box manufacturing plant to open a gas station and convenience store. Admittedly, working for family is tough. You spend all day working with your family members, all night with them at home, plus you have to take orders from them. Nonetheless, I wouldn't trade a single day of working with my family for anything in the world. These are some of the best memories in my life.

At the same time, I never closed the door of returning back to school. I still had law school in the back of my mind, but I wasn't sure whether I really wanted to actively pursue it or not. My family, on the other hand, always wanted me to become a lawyer, since they had a bigger vision for me (outside of working for our newly-created family business). Staying and working for the family business could have been my easy way out, but it would have kept me in our small community for the rest of my life. Through the constant support and push from my family, I never silenced the thought of returning back to school and leaving our town.

It still amazes me how my transition into the legal world came into existence. I remember the day vividly. I was sitting in my apartment in Pittsburgh, contemplating my next life move. I didn't know if school was the answer or if I had a different calling in life. That night, I did something that I didn't do regularly. I prayed! I asked Jesus to give me a sign as to what I should do. I can't make up what happened next. It shows how truly powerful and loving our Creator is. THE NEXT DAY, I took a drive from my apartment to my parents' house, which was about 35 miles. I had taken this route hundreds, if not thousands of times prior to this trip. I was familiar with all of the stores, restaurants, office buildings, schools, etc., on this route. But on this day, I noticed something drastically different.

There was a newly painted, bright red building with a large sign displayed in the front of the building. The sign had a white background with bold red letters that read, "SPINA LAW FIRM." I chuckled as I read these words because I simply couldn't believe my eyes. I looked up to the clouds and said, "Thank you, Jesus" for the literal sign that you placed in front of me. I filled out my application to take the LSAT (pre-exam for law school) and started doing research on law schools in Pennsylvania, New York, and Florida the next day.

MAKING A DIFFERENCE

Outside of working for my family, I did a little soul-searching during my two-year break from school to find out what I was truly passionate about. I realized that I enjoyed helping others get out of difficult situations, but I wasn't sure how I could turn that into something that would make a positive impact on my community. I had already gone to the source of the issues by hanging out with both drug users and dealers, but I wasn't successful in making any real change at that level.

One afternoon, my mother called me and asked if I wanted to attend a prescription drug abuse seminar that was being hosted at my alma mater, W&J, with her. She was attending on behalf of the medical office she was working for, so I decided to join her. While listening to the speakers, it was as if the Lord spoke directly to me through the men and women at the seminar, saying, "This is how you make a change." Sometimes, what you believe to be the root of the problem is actually just the stem. I realized that I was approaching the situation all wrong. I had the mistaken belief that if you could stop the drug dealers from supplying users with drugs (a very difficult task), then the users would find another "hobby."

Man... I was wrong! First off, addiction is not a hobby, it is a disease. If you have a friend or family member who is currently abusing narcotics, please remember that rehabilitation doesn't occur overnight. Addiction is like a cancer, which takes intensive treatment, support, and understanding to help cure. Please remember to remain selfless during this process. This isn't about you and has nothing to do with your emotions and/or disappointment in your loved one. It's about helping your loved one pull away from the strong grasp of this terrible disease.

After the seminar, I looked at my mother and said, "We need to bring this to our community!" That same day, we started to map out how this would work in our hometown, which had and still has a terrible heroin problem. To put it into perspective, I graduated high school in 2008 with less than 100 students in my graduating class. Now, in 2021, thirteen years removed from high school, I know more than 20 people from my school who have passed away from various causes and countless others that have overdosed, but survived. It's sad to see how strong of a grasp that drugs have on my community.

My mother and I began thinking of ways to combat this epidemic, but first, we needed to identify the root of the problem. The root of the problem was not the drug dealers supplying the drugs, or even the drugs themselves. It was the lack of knowledge that new users had, prior to experimenting with narcotics. Thus, we decided to launch the "Western Pennsylvania Prescription Drug Abuse Summit." It was a program that traveled to local high schools, middle schools, and even elementary schools around western Pennsylvania and was designed to educate students, teachers, parents, and community leaders on the dangers of prescription drug abuse.

Our research showed that most heroin users began using the drug due to a pre-existing dependency of prescription painkillers. These users would switch to heroin after their prescription was discontinued due to the high costs associated with the pills and their dependency on the drug to make them feel better. Therefore, we made it a point to educate the innocent youth before they fell into the trap of abusing prescription drugs. We found this to be the root of the problem, since you can't have an addiction to drugs if you never start abusing or using them in the first place.

We also hoped to deter people from experimenting with drugs, by educating them on the dangers associated with substance abuse. My mother and I realized that we needed a strong team around us, in order to make our program effective, so we formed a team that included local District Attorneys, the Pennsylvania Attorney General, members of the national and local DEA agencies, recovering addicts, coroners, drug and alcohol commissions, doctors, drug treatment centers, and local + state law enforcement officers.

Having a strong team is crucial to success. I think a lot of us try to be strong alone, but we need to remember that we are stronger together, especially when attempting to make a positive change. There really is power in numbers! In our first year, we traveled to more than seven school districts, holding three sessions at each school district: (1) a morning session for the students; (2) an afternoon session for the teachers, and; (3) an evening session open to parents and the local community. In our second year, we traveled to more than twelve schools! This journey led me to meet so many amazing people with tons of interesting and inspirational stories.

One story that I will never forget came from a young lady who spoke to the students at every one of our summits. This young lady, whom I will call Brittney to protect her identity, has a truly inspirational life journey and is the embodiment of hope, faith, and change. Brittney was broken, beaten, abused, and homeless. She was addicted to heroin, watched friends overdose and die right in front of her, became a convicted felon, and had been sexually assaulted many times. She talked about sleeping in cars, random hotels and motels, friends' houses, and even on the streets.

Brittney realized that she had a much larger calling in life than to remain shackled by this disease, so she sought help and made a full recovery. I'm proud to say that I know Brittney and that she has been drug-free for more than fifteen years! You may ask, "How is this possible?" "How did someone with such a terrible addiction, home-less, alone, beaten and abused turn her life around?" She stopped making excuses for herself! It is honestly that simple. She looked at herself in the mirror and said, "Today is the day I take responsibility for my actions."

Many of you reading this may think that you're alone, and that the mountain of success is too high to climb. But no matter what you are going through in life, no matter how difficult the road ahead looks, just remember what Brittney went through; how Brittney was able to take responsibility for her actions and not give up in the face of adversity; how Brittney was able to stop the excuses and own up to her mistakes, despite having all of the odds stacked against her. Now, Brittney is in a happy relationship, has a successful career, continues to help others on a daily basis, has a healthy daughter, and now has her felony charge expunged from her criminal record! Brittney is the embodiment of success!

Mistakes are a thing of the past! We must move past the mistakes that we once made, in order for us to have the future that we desire. Remember, we cannot change, alter, pause, or mold time, but we can envision and create our future!

6. The Move & Everything Changed

I DECIDED TO only visit one out of the four law schools that accepted me into their program. That school was St. Thomas University School of Law located in Miami, Florida. St. Thomas is a small, private, catholic school that's located (once again) in the "not-so-great" area of Miami, an area called Miami Gardens aka "Murder Gardens." "Something" told me that this was going to be my new home, and in 2014, I decided to pursue my legal path there. This was the first time that I lived more than an hour drive away from my family; little did I know of how difficult things were about to become.

Adjusting to law school was tough. It required hours upon hours of reading, writing, practicing, and memorizing. Once you get familiar with the laws then you have to learn how to apply them. One of the most famous answers that you'll hear a lawyer say is, "It depends," because it truly depends on the situation and facts when attempting to apply the law. I went countless nights without sleeping as I prepared for class the following morning. Yet, all of this was nothing compared to the test that the Lord was about to put in my path. I've always heard, "The Lord gives his strongest soldiers the most difficult tasks." I was about to find out just how strong my family really was.

I remember the day like it was yesterday. It was an October morning, muggy South Florida weather, and I had just gotten out of my Contracts class when I received a phone call from my mother that changed all of our lives forever. She asked if I was somewhere that I could talk. I told her that I was. This is the first time that I can vividly remember hearing my mother cry and not be able to control her emotions. She proceeded to tell me that they were at the doctor's office because my father had been having persistent headaches and small fevers over the last month or two. She stated that he was diagnosed with stage-four colon cancer, and that the doctors predicted that he only had five to fifteen days to survive.

My heart dropped into my stomach. My father, my hero, my business partner, my best friend, my idol was given an expiration date! I bawled my eyes out, crying uncontrollably as numerous friends attempted to calm me down. I will never forget hearing my mother say, "Please get on the next available flight to Pittsburgh. They are going to perform emergency surgery on your father tomorrow morning."

I couldn't help but think, "Why me?" "Why my father?" I thought this was all one terrible nightmare that I just couldn't seem to wake up from. Two of my best friends, Tanner Lakey and Samuel Rony, did everything in their powers to calm me down. More importantly, they were there with me and didn't leave me alone. Tanner actually spent the night at my apartment and drove me to the airport the next morning. He brought his video game system over, to keep us busy, and we stopped to grab snacks and Yoo-hoo from a local Walmart.

Looking back, I realized that asking the questions "why me?" and "why my father?" were selfish. I guess the better questions would have been, "why not me?" and "why not my father?" Remember, "The Lord gives his strongest soldiers the most difficult tasks." I took a second to reflect and quickly realized that the Lord had my family's back. It's quite an amazing story how my father's cancer was actually discovered in the first place. My mother had recently been named the CEO of a group of medical centers (a big jump from her position as a dental assistant when I was a child). She was home on her day off – a Sunday; a day when families commonly join together to celebrate the Lord. My parents were laying down, watching a movie, when one of the doctors from my mother's office called her because they were having issues with the computer system.

The doctor asked, "What are you doing?" She stated that she was home with my father because he was, "not feeling well again." The doctor asked, "What do you mean again?" My mother proceeded to tell him that he had a slight fever and headache every couple of days over the last several months, but would take an Advil and a quick nap, and then would wake up feeling much better.

The doctor asked my mother to bring him into the office first thing in the morning to get blood work. The doctor called my mother again, later that same evening, and asked her to go into a room by herself. He told my mother that he believed that my father had "lymphoma," which is a form of cancer that attaches to the body's lymph nodes. The incredible part – he hadn't even seen my father in person to run any sort of testing. This was simply his medical opinion, provided from only my mother's description over the phone and his "gut" instinct.

The next morning, my mother brought my father into the doctor's office. The diagnosis was colon cancer, which had also spread to his liver, lungs, and lymph nodes. The doctor said that it was so severe, that without treatment, he wouldn't have survived another five days! Even crazier, he told my mother that even with treatment, my father would likely only survive another sixty days. This was crushing news that I didn't know how to handle.

My entire family was devastated. Actually, my father was the only person who remained calm upon hearing everything. He told me, "The Lord knows when it's your time to go, and it's not my time to go yet." That next morning, I hopped on the first flight out of Miami and got to the hospital about 30 minutes before they took my father into the surgery room. We took 15 minutes alone as a family to just talk about everything. This was the first time that I ever saw my father cry. He was scared and couldn't hide that emotion any longer. I'll never forget the squeal that he let out as we all hugged one another; it sounded like a dying pig fighting for air. It was an emotionally crushing sound. My father, the man who I viewed as fearless, was now afraid.

Through it all, the Lord has always looked out for my family. My father was scheduled to have surgery on his liver and colon that day, in the hope of removing both tumors. However, hours before the surgery was scheduled to begin, the doctor walked into the room and said, "I've thought about this all night, and I've kept replaying the different scenarios in my head. I think that we'll go ahead and remove only the tumors in your colon today, and we'll schedule another surgery for

> "There is no medical reason why you are still alive."

your liver." This doctor, in particular, was a close family friend for years and he actually coached me in soccer as a teenager. We didn't second-guess his professional suggestion.

Thankfully, "something" told the doctor to make that decision, because, after the surgery, he told my family that if he had attempted to do both the colon and liver that day, there would have been an increased chance of my father not surviving the procedure. In fact, moving the liver surgery to a later date allowed for a liver specialist to come into town and perform the operation on my father. Needless to say, God watched over my father and guided the hands of the surgeon as he removed as much of the cancer from my father's body as he could. This didn't save my father's life, but it did prolong it!

Surgery after surgery, my father continued to disprove all medical opinions. One doctor actually stated, "There is no medical reason why you are still alive." It was at this point that I really started to discover Jesus and appreciate the power that He possesses.

CONTINUE WITH LIFE AS NORMAL, UNTIL …

In 2015, even with everything going on, I decided that I wanted to obtain my Master's in Business Administration (MBA), in addition to my Juris Doctorate degree. St. Thomas offered a joint degree program where students have the ability to graduate with their law degree and MBA in the same three-year period that you were expected to graduate with just your law degree. The only requirement to enter this program was the prerequisite of finishing your first year of law school. Then, during your second year, you'd begin to add MBA courses to

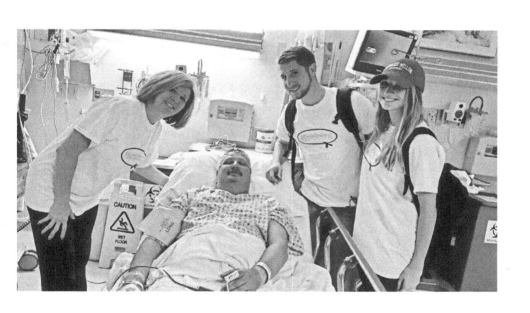

your schedule in the evenings until you finish the program.

My parents were extremely excited when I shared the news of my decision to enter into this program. They always believed that I was destined for something extraordinary, so I wanted to prove them right. I'll admit that it wasn't an easy time for me. My father was still battling cancer, I had my law school course load, I was volunteering at the Jason Taylor Foundation daily, began working at a sports agency (that I still work with) called Neostar Football, and then added MBA classes to my weekly schedule that took place from 6:00pm to 10:00pm three nights a week. I was also in a relationship with a girl that I met in law school and we were living together. Although I became very stressed at times, I felt extremely blessed that Jesus provided me with all of these opportunities. I also always kept the thought of my father - who never quit or gave up - in the back of my mind; regardless of how stressed I became, it provided me with the strength to go on.

> "We can either feel sorry for ourselves and dwell on the situation that we're in, or we can push through the situation and become stronger than ever."

Tough times are a test of our strength. We can either feel sorry for ourselves and dwell on the situation that we're in, or we can push through the situation and become stronger than ever. Life is like a game of poker; we can't control the cards that we're dealt. Most of the time, we can't control the events that will occur in our life, but we do have the power to determine how we handle those events. Feeling sorry for ourselves wastes valuable time. We need to embrace the challenges that life throws at us and use distractors as fuel to move forward; not as shackles holding us down. Life doesn't stop because it becomes difficult, so, stand up and fight!

Fighting was something that I was used to. I had been fighting my entire life. So, during my first semester of law school, I had to fight again; fight to break into the sports industry! Getting your foot in the door is extremely difficult in sports. It seemed like no matter what I did, I couldn't land a position with a sports agency. I called different agents and agency groups every single day, and oftentimes, I circled back with the agents.

There was one group in particular that I did everything I could think of to gain their attention. I called and texted the agent every day, for about two months. I sent weekly emails with updates, liked all of their social media posts, and even sent my resume to their office on several occasions. I prayed and asked God to please help me secure a position with this agency because I believed that landing the job would ultimately shape my future of becoming one of the most successful agents in sports history... or at least give me a jump start.

Finally, after months of trying, I received a call from one of the agents in the agency. My heart fell into my stomach when I saw the agent's name pop up on my phone. This was it! This was my opportunity literally calling me. I answered the call, and the agent said, "Sam, we have thousands of applicants from all over the country every single year. We get messages from law students at Harvard, Yale, etc., who want an opportunity to work with us, but we have never experienced someone as persistent as you. You really stuck out to us."

At this point, I was thinking, "Wow! God, you answered my prayers again!" Then he said, "But right now, we are not looking to expand our operations. In fact, we are looking to downsize. Now Sam, I have a strong feeling that you will do well in whatever you decide to do in life. Some things in life you cannot control. In fact, most things in life you cannot control, but you can either choose to run into the wall in front of you or run around it."

That message - despite that it deprived me of my dream opportunity - has stuck with me ever since that day. He was right! Why run into a wall when you can run around it? Just like my story earlier about when I played football. I didn't need to run into the two big linebackers full-speed again. I needed to pivot and find a different path. It was the closing of only one opportunity, and if I would have let that define me, then I would have deprived myself of so many more. The Lord had a different path for me; this is something we must all learn to embrace. Life doesn't always happen to the exact specifications as we hope, but that doesn't mean we should completely abandon our path. We must just take an alternative route to reach our final destination.

7. The Fight Continues

MY FATHER CONTINUED to battle cancer for more than two and a half years. For those of you who are starting this journey with a loved one, I have a piece of advice for you. Expect to experience a rollercoaster of emotions! There will be many highs and many lows, but the three most important things you can do are: (1) pray; (2) stay positive even though it will be difficult to do so; and (3) cherish every moment that you have together here on earth.

At one point, it looked as if my father had achieved something doctors believed to be impossible. A man who had a five to sixty-day expiration date was now over a year into his fight. He had colon, liver, and lymph node surgeries. He had countless chemotherapy and radiation treatments. Finally, one of his scans came back essentially clean! It looked as if he had beaten the terrible disease and I remember thanking Jesus over and over again for working yet another miracle in my family's life. My sister and I made signs saying, "CANCER FREE," and hung them around our house. But the one thing about cancer is that the battle is never over. You must always remain ready for the unknown.

About a month later, my mother called me and said that my father was acting a little different. She stated that he was being very abrupt with his responses to people, seemed on edge or irritable at all times, would yell at people (something he would NEVER do), and wasn't eating very much. Then, one day, when they were leaving dinner, the Lord provided us with another sign. My father started to stumble out of the restaurant, and almost fell over due to his loss of balance. My mother said that he looked drunk and couldn't stand up straight on his own. At this point, she forced him back into the doctor's office where they ran several tests.

Once again, I can remember this day as if it happened yesterday. My mother called me in the morning, before I walked into class, to tell me that she was taking my father in for another check-up. I had a knot in my stomach after that phone call; I remember telling my girlfriend that "something" didn't feel right and that I had a feeling I would be flying home the next day.

That "something" was Jesus preparing me for the news that I never expected to hear. Approximately twenty minutes after class ended, I received a call from my mother as I was walking to my car in the school's parking lot. She sounded nervous. I could tell that she was seriously panicking and even crying. This was the second time I had ever heard my mother cry - as she is a strong woman - so I assumed the worst. She proceeded to tell me that my father's cancer came back and had spread to his brain.

I couldn't breathe ...

I fell to my knees in the school parking lot, picked myself up, and sat on the trunk of my car. The war that my father had just won was now back with a new army... and it was stronger than before. I boarded a flight and flew home the next morning to be with my family, since my father was having emergency brain surgery that day. The doctors were shocked that he hadn't already suffered a stroke; "something" unknown to them had prevented it from happening. Once again, my father defied modern medicine.

By the time my flight landed and I got into a car, I made it to the hospital about an hour before his surgery. He was calm and had a smile on his face when I arrived. When I asked him if he was scared, he said, "No. God knows when it's your time to go and it's not my time yet." He always had faith in Jesus, especially during these challenging moments.

During the procedure, the doctors came out and warned my family that when my dad comes out of the surgery, he may not remember all of our names right away, could have verbal and cognitive issues for a few days, and will need therapy to help him learn how to walk properly again. Once again, Jesus worked one of His miracles on my father.

My mother, my sister, and I walked into his room in the ICU unit of the hospital about 30 minutes after he got out of surgery. It was the first NFL game of the year for the Pittsburgh Steelers, and their star running back, Le'Veon Bell was suspended for the first few games, due to violating the NFL's substance abuse policy, so, DeAngelo Williams replaced him at the running back position. We started off by asking my father simple questions to test his recovery. My mother asked him if he knew who she was and he responded with her name. I asked him if he knew who I was and he responded with my name. Then my sister asked him if he knew who she was. He got quiet. He was staring aimlessly into space. We all got nervous. My sister looked like she had just seen a ghost and had her heart broken at the exact same time.

Suddenly, my father looked at me and said, "Sammy did you see that run by Williams?" I remember thinking, "Is this real life right now? A man who is an hour out of intensive brain surgery is cognitive enough to watch a football game and recognize that their star running back is not playing in the game." I am still astonished by this. Needless to say, he didn't experience any memory loss from the surgery, and he ended up answering my sister's question that he knew who she was.

Later that evening, my father began to pull the cords and tubes out of his body. When the nurses ran into his room to ask what he was doing, my father said, "I want to walk. The faster that I can show you that I can walk and get back onto my feet, the faster I can get out of here." There he was, the strongest man I know, wanting to fight and win this seemingly impossible battle. Who was I or any doctor to tell him that the fight was impossible? He had the belief and strength necessary to take on this challenge. Plus, he was fearless in the face of adversity.

Instead of fearing death and giving up hope, he remained positive, looked "impossible" in the face, and went straight at this disease with everything that he had. I still have the video of my father waking up the morning after his brain surgery and walking down the hall. At the end of the hall, he turned to a door and said, "I want you to watch me walk up those stairs." The nurse didn't like the idea, but as my father persisted, the nurse said, "Okay, you can go up a couple of steps." My father walked up one full flight of steps (twelve total steps) to the first landing and back down. This amazed me and showed me strength that I never knew existed. His positive mindset allowed him to accomplish much more than most medical experts perceived as possible.

I attribute the longevity of my father's life to his continuous positive outlook on life every single morning that he woke up. In those two and a half years during his battle, I learned how big of a blessing it is to wake up each and every day and also how fragile life itself is. The only things guaranteed are death and disappointment, but having a positive attitude will enhance your enjoyment and outlook of life. That's one of the main points that I want you to take from my father's battle. He could have easily felt sorry for himself, depressed, scared, and stayed in bed all day every day, but what would that have done? It would have sped up his death. The same goes for you in whatever adversity you're currently battling! If you can learn or even force yourself to keep a positive outlook on the situation, I promise that it will get better.

Battling cancer is a tiresome, grueling, and heart-wrenching process. Some believe that it is actually more difficult on the family than it is on the person going through it. Expect to hear news that you do not wish to hear. Expect to spend six or more hours in a doctor's office for every chemotherapy treatment. Expect the unexpected, but always remember to cherish the time you have with that person. Depending on how you perceive the situation, this process can either be a blessing or a burden. Admittedly, I initially thought this to be a large burden on the life of my family and I, but I now realize how big of a blessing this all was.

My family is closer than ever because of all of the hospital visits, surgeries, chemotherapy, radiation treatments, and uniform prayers that we would proclaim every night. I was given a chance to witness, first-hand, the strength that one man can possess. Seeing my father never complain, never take pain medication (even after his surgeries), defy all medical expert opinions, and do it all with a smile on his face are the most amazing things I have ever witnessed.

For these reasons, my relationship with Jesus has never been stronger, and I'm very thankful for that. Before this battle started, I did not pray on a daily basis, rarely attended church, and almost went down the wrong path at different stages in my life. Now, I talk with Jesus several times a day, attend and serve at church on a regular basis, and truly hope that I can inspire others who are going through a difficult time to find peace in Him.

8. New Job

AS I MENTIONED earlier, even with everything going on, I still found time to volunteer on a daily basis at the Jason Taylor Foundation. The Foundation was my first real "in" to the sports world. I saw it as a "win-win" situation, since I was able to continue my passion of helping others through volunteering at the Foundation while simultaneously being exposed to different aspects of the sports industry.

People who want to work in the sports industry ask me how to get started since this is a very difficult industry to break into. Truthfully, there is no clear-cut answer. I've heard hundreds (if not thousands) of stories about how executives, agents, and other business professionals got started in the sports world, yet, my story was unlike any of the ones that I have heard. My start was by fate, chance, creativity, and persistence. I didn't have a relative or best friend who played professional football. I didn't come from a wealthy family who could provide financial backing for me while I chased my dreams of becoming an NFL agent.

I didn't have a lot of tools that many other agents had when breaking into the industry, but I did have faith. I did have persistence. I did have a positive mindset, which enabled me to embrace each opportunity that I came across. I did have the desire to make a difference in a young man's life.

One of the first steps I took was becoming Vice President of my law school's Entertainment and Sports Law Society (ESLS). Our ESLS program planned to host an event with the Miami Dolphins where we took our student-members to a Dolphins game. We talked with the Dolphins' staff and set up a meeting with the team's legal counsel prior to the start of the game. All of our ESLS members were extremely excited for the opportunity, but I wanted more. I wanted Miami Dolphins legend, Defensive End, Jason Taylor to meet with us as well. This all occurred approximately six months before I started working with Jason's foundation, and I had never met Jason.

A buddy of mine, Dante, that went to W&J with me was in town to visit me, so I told him about my plan to try to meet with Jason. Ironically, he went to high school and played football with Jason's younger brother. I asked Dante to make the introduction, and he did so that same day. I called Jason's brother and he instructed me to contact Jason's foundation director – a man named Seth Levit. I called Seth every week (sometimes multiple times a week), asking him to help coordinate Jason to speak with our students at the Dolphins game. Unfortunately, the plan didn't work out, but shortly after this experience, I began volunteering at the foundation.

Seth knew from day one that I wanted to become an NFL agent and work with athletes, so he helped me gain experience any way that he could. Around that same time, he started scheduling speaking engagements for Jason and let me tag along to gain experience in the sports marketing world.

Ironically, Jason's Foundation shared an office with a company called Neostar Sports and Entertainment. Neostar's founder and President, Ralph Stringer has been the representative for Hall of Fame Quarterback Dan Marino for more than thirty-five years. At the time, Neostar no longer represented current athletes and had turned its efforts toward the marketing and business ventures for their retired clients. Knowing my desire to become and NFL agent, Ralph and I communicated on a regular basis. He provided me with knowledge, insight, and opportunities.

Entering the sports industry is extremely difficult, and there is no clear path on how to break in. While still volunteering with the Foundation, I began asking and helping Ralph with small side projects (mostly research). One day, one of his employees took me to lunch and told me that he accepted a position with another company and would be leaving Neostar. He suggested that I speak with Ralph to see if I could fill his position. I remember calling my father with excitement and telling him of my plan to apply for this new opening.

A few weeks later (days before the employee left), I drafted a well-thought-out email proposal and application (with the help of Seth) in the hope of filling the newly opened position. Days later, Ralph called me into his office to discuss my proposal. He said, "Sam, I'm actually not looking to fill the position. In fact, I'm not really looking to stay in the sports side of the business much longer. I want to branch into more business-oriented projects moving forward, and have been transitioning into this over the past several years." Again, I had been shut down, trying to enter the sports world. "Something" about this one felt different though, and I knew this was not how it was supposed to end.

That could have been the end of my story. I could have taken that answer and just continued volunteering with the Foundation as I started down a career path geared toward becoming a criminal defense attorney, which is what I initially wanted to be when I started law school. Instead, when the employee left, I moved all of my stuff into his office and started answering the phone as people would call the office. Admittedly, I was nervous at first, since I didn't know how Ralph would react, but I didn't want to let this opportunity slip through my fingertips. Luckily, after a few weeks, I think Ralph started to realize that "this guy isn't going anywhere" and began to slowly embrace my vision for Neostar.

Ralph provided me with some of the greatest memories and opportunities I've had in life. He taught me countless life lessons that I'll take with me no matter where I am in this world. His generosity, reputation in the industry, and compassionate personality have truly inspired me. I am forever grateful to Jesus for directing me into his path. I mean what are the odds that I would start volunteering at the Foundation that shares the same office as Ralph; an office where one employee decided to leave a few months after I began volunteering? Furthermore, Ralph embraced me moving into his office, despite that he initially shut me down ... multiple times! "Somehow," this storybook situation occurred and I'm forever thankful. Ralph has and will forever be a mentor in my life.

But, just because Ralph now accepted me to work at Neostar didn't mean that my fight was over. I still had to convince Ralph to get back into the active representation of athletes' business, since that was what I wanted to do. Ralph fought with me on this for months, stating, "Are you sure that you want to enter into this space? It's a tough industry." I had already made up my mind at this point; I was all in, so I went to work on Ralph, slowly, but steadily.

I knew that I couldn't do this alone, so I had a ton of conversations with some of our retired clients such as Dan Marino, Jason Taylor, OJ McDuffie, Dwight Stephenson, Joe Rose, and several others. Then one day, Dan and Ralph looked at me and said, "You should speak with Marvin Demoff."

Marvin Demoff was Dan's NFLPA Contract Advisor. He is a legend in NFL circles, and is arguably the best agent to ever represent NFL athletes. To date, Marvin has more than 13 athletes who have been inducted into the Pro Football Hall of Fame, such as Dan Marino, John Elway, Troy Polamalu, Jonathan Ogden, Shannon Sharpe, and the late Junior Seau, to name a few.

He's also the only agent to ever have an "ESPN 30 for 30" documentary film done on him, titled, *Elway to Marino*, which highlights the 1983 NFL Draft through Marvin's point of view. Marvin represents several athletes from that draft class, including first round picks: Elway, Marino, Eric Dickerson, and Jimbo Covert.

Needless to say, I was fired up when Dan and Ralph brought up this opportunity. We set up a call, and Marvin spoke with me for nearly forty minutes. At the end of the call, he said, "Come to LA anytime, and the office will be open for you." That's all that I needed to hear. I responded back with, "Thank you, Marvin. I will see you tomorrow." Yes, I booked the next flight out of Miami to Los Angeles and spent the entire week out there with Marvin. By the end of my trip, he told me, "I'm here to help you with whatever you need."

BOOM! My team was starting to fall into place. Ralph and Marvin were now reunited as senior consultants to my youthful energy, which I used to hustle and get in front of people.

Working in the sports industry enabled me to provide my father with an opportunity that many others would not have had the ability to do. One morning, I asked Dan if he could get me in contact with someone in the Pittsburgh Penguins organization to see if I could present my father with the opportunity to meet Mario Lemieux, an NHL legend and the owner of the Penguins. My father enjoyed watching all sports, but hockey was by far his favorite. He wouldn't miss a Penguins game, even if that meant listening to it on the radio while he was doing something else. Every day, about six to seven times a day, my father and I would talk on the phone. Nearly every single one of those conversations involved hockey or some sort of Pittsburgh sports talk.

Graciously, Dan called one of his friends, former NHL great Pierre ("Lucky Pierre") Larouche and asked him to contact me. One day, while I was in New York City, I received a call from Pierre who stated that he spoke with Dan and asked me how he could help out. I told him about my father's current medical state and passion for the Penguins. Pierre said, "Well, Mario is out of town, but I share a suite with him at the games. How about I leave you two tickets to watch the game with me in the Penguins' owner's suite?" Pierre, words cannot describe how much this moment meant to both me and my father.

I ended up taking my father to watch the Pittsburg Penguins play the New York Rangers in the Penguins' owner's suite just days before Christmas. I had never seen my father that excited in his life. Every time somebody walked into the suite, my father would turn to me and say, "Sam, that's the TV announcer. Sam, that's the general manager. Sam, that's ..." It felt like I took him to his first ever sporting event and he was surrounded by his idols. It gave me chills because my father wasn't the type of person who got easily excited. In fact, he rarely displayed emotion. That's what made it so special to see him act like a little kid in a candy store; that's something I will never forget. It's an indescribable feeling to witness your father have the best day of his life, while watching his favorite team play, and knowing that, me, his son helped make that day possible.

> "You shouldn't live a life of "what if's.?" Live a life of attempts. Live a life of accomplishments."

After the game, Pierre took us down to the Penguins' locker room to meet the players where team captain, Sidney Crosby, greeted my father. Sidney asked my father what he thought of the game and proceeded to give him a full tour of the locker room. Once again, to see the look of excitement on my father's face is something that I will cherish forever.

You hear stories of how sports can impact lives all around the world. For me, it was amazing to see this unfold first hand. Prior to the game, my father was not eating a lot because his chemotherapy and radiation treatments were killing his appetite and making him feel nauseous. He was losing weight at a rapid pace and was afraid to eat in public since he didn't want to throw up.

That was one of the most difficult side effects associated with cancer and I hated to see my father battle through that. Yet, the morning following the game, my father woke up and ate two bowls of cereal. It was amazing to see how a short jolt of excitement could really affect his health. I was amazed to see the type of energy my father had the morning after the game. I sat on the couch, thanking Jesus for answering this prayer; it ended up being one evening that I will never forget. It's crazy to look back and think that I almost didn't ask for the opportunity.

If there is one characteristic that I possess, it's that I hate asking for anything. I don't like handouts, feeling reliant on another person, or asking for favors. But in this situation, I'm forever grateful that "something" told me to ask for this particular favor. If you ever have the opportunity during your lifetime to do something special for someone, something ordinarily not possible for that particular person, or just something that you believe will make someone's day, please put your pride to the side and just ask. The worst response you will hear is the word "no."

Having a fear of hearing a negative response will haunt you for the rest of your life. You shouldn't live a life of "what if's?" Live a life of attempts. Live a life of accomplishments. If you fail, find a different angle or way to approach the situation. Luckily, my request didn't fail, and I didn't need to seek an alternative route in this particular situation, but I do believe that if it had failed, I would have found a way to do something special for my father.

I'm beyond blessed and grateful for everything Ralph, Dan, Pierre, and Sidney did to make this dream a reality for my father. I'm forever grateful.

9. The Last Exhale

AS TIME WENT on, my father's cancer continued to get stronger. His health began to decline at a rapid pace. That's the scary part with cancer that I wasn't prepared for. He went from driving to work every day to, in a week, not being able to leave his bed on his own the next. He started to have trouble walking, and began using a walking cane. Still, through everything, his response was always the same, "I am fine." My father never wanted anyone to see him struggle, especially his kids. He was a proud man who never wanted to feel dependent or weak.

But the thing is, you can't hide weakness when your body is literally shutting down. The first time I really noticed that his health was declining was the day he needed help making it up the stairs. We were walking into our house from a quick trip to the supermarket when I noticed how slow he was moving when he reached the stairs. His legs had weakened due to his malnutrition and he was having a difficult time making it up each step. The emotions that I felt in this moment are hard to describe. All along, I thought this man was Superman and could overcome anything in his path. I mean, this was the same man who walked up a flight of stairs the morning after his first brain surgery for crying out loud!

But this time, something was different. He held onto my shoulder as we approached the last step and turned to me to ask if I could help lift him over the final step. I'll never forget the look of embarrassment in his eyes as he asked me that question. He looked helpless, sad, and ashamed that he had to rely on his son's help to make it up the stairs. After getting him to the couch, I walked into a separate room, and tears instantly ran down my face.

I remember telling myself, "This is okay. He's just not feeling well because of the radiation that he's receiving, but he'll be back to normal after his final treatment." Meanwhile, deep down, I knew that this wasn't true. I was attempting to mask my emotions with false hope and wanted to find comfort in something so uncomfortable that no living species could even fake comfort in.

After a few weeks, I started to get used to seeing him with the walking cane. He would always crack jokes about it to lighten the mood. That's another thing that I'll always admire about my father; no matter how scared he was or how dark the situation looked, he would always find a light to help guide us all through the darkness. He always trusted in the Lord to guide him through his difficult times. He told me, "It's your perspective on the situation that truly determines whether it's good or bad." Sometimes, he would also say things like, "It can always be worse." I used to think, "How could it be any worse?" He had a brain tumor, colon cancer, lung cancer, lymphoma, and liver cancer. Yet, he always had a smile on his face because he truly appreciated each and every morning that he woke up.

As he kept fighting, so did the disease. His weakened immune system left holes in his armor, which allowed bacteria to creep in. He was diagnosed with pneumonia, and this was a huge scare for all of us. He started taking medication and, as he always seemed to do, he beat it. The first time…

The pneumonia came back a couple of weeks later. At this point, I was flying home every Friday, then back to Miami on Sunday afternoons. I continued this trend for about a month. Shortly after, the pneumonia got worse and my father was hospitalized. As I mentioned earlier, my father never wanted anyone to feel sorry for him, so, every time I flew home to see him, he would immediately check to make sure that I wasn't missing class. I remember one time when he pulled out his phone, while in the hospital bed, to book me a return flight back to Miami; this was a day before his first brain surgery. He was so confident that everything was going to be okay that he didn't want my education to suffer. My education and future were important to him, so he wanted to make sure that I was there, handling my business. The last thing he wanted was for his disease to disrupt mine or my sister's future. That's just the type of man that he was.

When I first arrived at the hospital, he was excited to see me, yet, I could tell that something was different this time around. He was struggling to catch his breath due to the pneumonia and had trouble speaking, because every time he spoke, he would start to cough. Since he didn't want to take any medication, my mother asked the nurse to provide him with small doses of morphine to relax him and hopefully, control his cough a little. When he found out what my mother had requested from the nurse, he was shockingly happy instead of angry. The morphine was making him feel comfortable and relaxed.

Reality sank in the next morning. I asked my father, "So, I need to book my flight back to Miami for class. Do you think I should go back tomorrow or wait one more day?" For the first time ever, he said, "Why don't you just stay?" At this moment, I knew it was happening. I knew that he came to the realization that he was not going to make it out of this hospital bed. Like he always said, "You know when it's your time." Clearly, he knew that this was his time to go and he wanted his whole family to be there with him.

If any of you reading this ever experience a moment like this, please, cherish every second that you have remaining with that loved one. It will be the most gratifying and difficult time of your life. Try not to selfishly start crying and walk out of the room. I know that it's difficult to control your emotions, but trust me, you will cherish these moments for the rest of your life. I remember sitting in his room as he fell asleep, and hiding my head so that he couldn't see me crying. I felt lost, confused, and lonely, even though he was lying in the bed next to me. It started to feel as if he was already gone, even though he was still present. I can't really explain the feeling any other way, it was just a surreal realization of what was about to occur.

Slowly, the nurses began to increase my father's morphine as the pneumonia grew stronger. It got to a point where he could no longer keep his eyes open and he eventually fell into a deep sleep. If this happens to someone you love, know that he/she can hear every word you are saying, even though he/she is not conscious. You may not get a reaction from the person, but trust me, they can hear every word that you say. Speak to your loved one. Say anything and everything that you want him or her to hear before they take that dreaded final breath.

I had this exact moment with my father. For years, I had been self-ishly praying for my father to keep fighting so that he could witness my law school graduation. But in this moment, while watching him suffer, watching him gasp for air, and seeing his chest and head moving and jolting backwards as he attempted to inhale, I found myself praying for something different. I prayed for him to just let go and for him to finally have the peace that he deserved. I asked Jesus to grant one more prayer for my father, "Please take my father to Your heavenly gates and let him enter peacefully."

My family gave me five minutes alone with my father. I told him everything that I ever wanted to tell him. I made him promises that I plan to keep forever. I held his hand, gave him a kiss on his forehead, and said, "It's okay to let go now. I love you so much man, but you deserve to be at peace. Mom, Mara, and I will be okay. Go, see your father and my grandma. I love you man." I left the room as my sister and mother each had their time alone with him. Afterwards, the three of us went to eat lunch down the hall from his room.

We returned to his room about thirty minutes later. When we walked in, he was noticeably a different color. The nurse said this is called "mottling," and it occurs when a person starts to slowly die. At this point, my mother, my sister, and I asked everyone to please leave the room. I held his right hand while my mother and sister held his left hand. My father's breaths started to have longer and longer gaps between them. We all told him, "We love you, but please do not try to hold on any longer. You have been strong for so long." At this point, while holding onto his hands, my father exhaled for the last time.

Seeing my father take that last breath is the most difficult thing

I've ever experienced. I wanted to scream and be silent at the same time. I wanted to curl up into a ball and run around the hospital at the same time. I wanted to be alone, yet, with everyone at the same time. My mind felt as if it departed from my skull and I was watching myself walk through the motions. I remember calling Kory, Nick, Geno, Sam, Tanner, Matt, and Zach, even though I knew that they wouldn't have an answer for me. The truth is, there is no comfort in seeing someone you love take their last breath other than realizing that the person is now serving in Heaven with our Lord.

At this time, my emotions were everywhere. I didn't know what to do. Yet, for "some reason," I felt a calming feeling take over my body. I realized that Jesus once again answered my prayer and that my father was now at peace. He had suffered for more than two and a half years, but during that time, he inspired countless people.

One particular instance that comes to mind was my father's friendship with a local high school student. The student found out that he had bone cancer and would need several painful surgeries to treat his disease. My father - even though he had his own battle to worry about - dropped everything to be there with the kid during the kid's first chemotherapy treatment. They would talk on a weekly basis and remained close friends over the years. Even at our family's convenience store, customers would approach my father and ask him for advice, which he would gladly share with everyone. He was always positive, smiling, joking, and caring.

As difficult and numbing of an experience this may be for you, please attempt to count your blessings throughout the process. This experience was secretly a blessing for my father. He had suffered for so long and was now selected to come to heaven early to serve our God. I came to the understanding that God didn't take my father to make my family grieve at his departure from earth. No, it was the opposite. He brought my father to heaven because He realized that my father had finished his work on earth, and is destined for something much greater, during his eternal life.

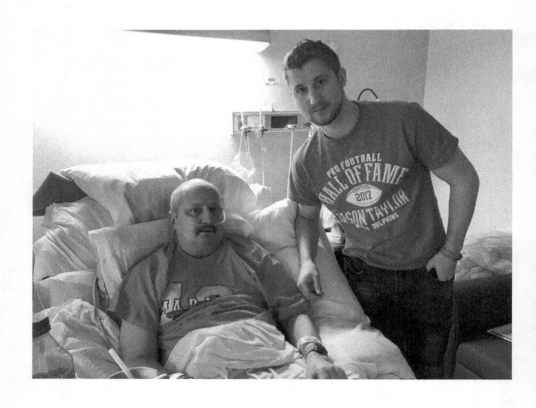

When a person dies, it's amazing to see the amount of support people give. It's a true statement to one's life when you witness how many people actually care about that person. Seeing all of the people at my father's funeral showed me how great and inspirational of a man he truly was. We had a viewing service scheduled from 6:00pm to 8:00pm, but we didn't end up leaving the funeral home until approximately 10:30pm that evening.

Thousands of people showed up from all over to pay their final respect to MY FATHER. There were people who waited in line (outside in 35-degree weather) for over an hour to come say goodbye to this amazing man. The funeral director stated that this was the largest funeral he had ever seen. It truly is a blessing.

The following passage is the speech that I read to our friends and family in attendance at the church the morning of my father's funeral:

For those of you who know my father well, it's only fitting to have written this on my phone.

First, my family and I want to thank you all for coming out this morning, not to mourn the death of my father, but to celebrate his life. I'm sure most of you in here have a story about my father and that he served some role in your life, whether he was your coach, mentor or friend.

Whether you remember him for one of his corny jokes like calling Nicholas, Pennyless or some other type of event, the one thing about my father that I will always remember is that he was always there.

It didn't matter if it was a soccer, football, or hockey game. Cheerleading event, boxing match, or whatever other endeavor my sister or I wished to enter into … he was always there.

It also didn't matter the time of day or night, whether he had slept or not, whether there was something else that he could have been doing… he was always there.

Selfishly, I do wish my father would have been able to make it another month to witness my graduation, since him being there has been something I've grown so comfortable with, but I started thinking last night, and realize that he will not only be there with my family and I, he will have the best seat in the house.

He will be sitting next to me on that stage.

He will be walking with me to receive that diploma. And more importantly, he will be with my family no matter where we decide to go in life.

You see, one of the things I've learned through all of this is that it's extremely difficult to find someone on this earth who does not have an enemy somewhere out there –someone that everyone enjoys their presence and someone you will never hear a bad word about.

It's amazing and an honor to call one of those few men my father; a man who I will always proudly share a name with.

You see, my father's only enemy in life was the one he was battling within; the evil cancer that caused so much suffering. My dad always preached that it's your perspective on life that differentiates whether a situation is good or bad; a win from a loss.

Now, while many of us in here today believe that he lost the battle with cancer, I think he actually won the war.

He defied all odds and medical opinions. He walked my sister down the aisle on her wedding day.

He did so much within a two-and-a-half-year span that most people would not even dream possible in a lifetime.

My father embraced his situation, he did not fear it, and because of his fearless attitude, I truly believe he was victorious.

Quick story. Days before my father passed, while he was lying there in his hospital bed, he was still in high spirits joking around. My mother said to him, "What do you say to me?" He said, "I love you." My sister said, "What about me?" He responded, "I love you more." Then I asked, "Well, what about me?" He responded, "I love you more more." Then my sister said, "What about Matt (her husband)?" My father responded, "Stupid idiot," which had been an inside joke from earlier that week. He always kept his spirits high.

Dad, I will always love you. You've left behind an amazing family that will continue to make you proud. Mom, Mara, Stupid Idiot, and I will always have you with us and I truly know you will always be there. Thank you for everything.

THE WAVES WERE HUGE

After the passing of my father, I was confused, sad, and distraught. He was my best friend, my idol, my hero, and so much more. But I knew that I had to continue marching forward. I had my last semester of law school final exams less than a month away and needed to focus. I couldn't afford to waste time grieving any longer because I knew that I couldn't get that time back... plus my father would be disappointed if I let my school work suffer. I decided to buckle down and grind to ensure that I would graduate law school and obtain my Master's degree within that month. I had a promise to fulfill to my hero.

Jesus has a funny way of showing us our capabilities. I kept repeating to myself, "God gives His strongest soldiers the most difficult tasks." I wanted to prove to my father, my family, and myself that I was one of His strongest soldiers. I've learned that you never have to prove anything to Jesus since He already knows the answer, but you do have to show Him that you have an understanding of His message. You have to show Him that you believe everything He is doing has a much larger meaning than we can comprehend on this earth.

> "Life is about perspective. You can make any positive situation negative and any negative situation positive."

Life is about perspective. You can make any positive situation negative and any negative situation positive. I realized that I was being sad for selfish reasons. I was sad because my father was no longer physically present on this earth. I was sad because I would not be able to speak with him every day on the telephone. I was sad for all of the wrong reasons because I never once stopped to think about how peaceful my father had now become; how much pain and suffering he endured on a daily basis; how hard it was for him to come to terms with reality and accept the fact he was leaving his family behind on this earth.

While in his hospital room, I wrote in my phone's notebook a few times, as a coping mechanism for all of my emotions. At one point, I wrote, "Watching him suffer and gasp for air was the hardest thing I've ever had to do." At that moment in time, when I wrote this sentence, I was feeling pain for the man who was attempting to stay alive for my selfish reasons. I understood that he was dealing with pain and suffering, yet, the minute he took that last breath, all selflessness turned right back into selfishness. I needed to re-group and clear my head because I knew that I needed to trust the Lord.

In the book of Acts Chapter 27, Paul was sailing to Rome when the boat he was on encountered an extremely violent storm with hurricane-like winds. Paul and the others aboard the ship were scared, but Paul kept faith throughout. Even though Paul was a prisoner on the ship, he was still a leader. He kept the other prisoners calm, convinced everyone to eat after fourteen days of starving and eventually led the passengers to the safety of land on an island known as Malta. Paul embraced the waves that were thrown at him, which is something we should all learn how to do. He could have gone into a corner and hid due to the fear that he was facing, but instead, he embraced the fear, turned it into energy, and helped save the lives of many. Paul could have let fear define him, and that would have ultimately led to an early departure from earth, but he didn't.

Fear can either define you or make you stronger. Paul, unlike his companions on the ship, used fear to make him a stronger person. Just when it seemed like all hope was lost, Paul became stronger than ever. He didn't want to let fear ruin or control his life here on earth, thus, he took his fear and molded it into success. This was something that I needed to do. I had this fear of the unknown. The fear of losing my father. The fear of losing my idol. The fear of walking through the rest of my life without my guide. Yet, I always had and will have a guide. His name is Jesus. I needed to turn this fear and selfishness into positive energy that I could use to help others; that I could use to help my family; that I could use to help myself fulfill all of those goals that I had set forth.

When life puts waves in your path and you become afraid, don't panic! It's natural to become fearful, but you need to learn how to take that fear and turn it into something far greater than you could ever imagine. Take that pain you are feeling and use it to create comfort for others. For me, I found comfort in Jesus who helped me stay on my chosen path. I was able to take this fear and convert it into positive energy; energy that I used in school to make sure I still graduated on time; energy to comfort my mother and sister; energy to serve at my church in Miami; energy to make sure that I showed up to take the Florida Bar Exam and my NFL agent exam, which were four days apart in two separate states. Finally, I used this energy to finish this book so that I can hopefully help at least one person through whatever it is that he/she is currently going through.

FAITHFUL FOR THE UNFAITHFUL

This book is not an attempt to force anyone to dedicate his or her life to Jesus Christ. However, it is my hope that if you are going through a difficult time in your life, are in need of someone to talk with and are too embarrassed to ask a friend or someone in your family for guidance, and/or believe that you're walking through life alone, that you realize Jesus is always with you.

There were times throughout my journey where I found myself losing faith. I found myself second-guessing the power of our Lord. I found myself lost, confused, and lonely. But even with my knowledge and belief in Jesus, I constantly found myself running away from Him instead of leaning toward him. I found myself drifting in the opposite direction of safety even though the current was pulling me toward His grasp.

I'm not sure why I constantly pushed away from "something" that provided so much comfort to me, but sometimes in life, you must discover your faith before you can discover yourself. Once you are able to discover your faith, realize you are never alone, and trust in the Lord, then you will be ready to tackle whatever challenges life throws your way. This, at least, is what happened to me.

In today's world, there are a lot of people who don't believe in Jesus because they've never "seen" Him. Many of these same individuals believe they are witnessing moments in life, yet, haven't put their cellphones down long enough to lift their eyes to the sky. I believe there is a monstrous difference between witnessing something and simply watching it occur. You can watch many things in life, but that does not necessarily mean you are witnessing them. Watching is simply observing. It's like going to the same desk each and every day in school or at work. You don't appreciate the desk (usually, you despise it since it reminds you of some sort of work) even though you see it on a regular basis.

On the other hand, you don't need to see something to witness it. Right now, you are probably reading this and thinking that I am crazy (and maybe I am) but hear me out. Think of the blind man or woman who has never seen the green grass, blue ocean, blue sky, or palm trees. That person may have never seen that item, place, or color before, yet, that person can still witness it since he or she believes they are in its presence. That person believes they are surrounded by that item or in that place and can feel the energy associated with their surroundings.

Similarly, imagine a blind man or woman at an NBA Finals basketball game. He or she may not be able to see what is occurring, but that person can certainly feel the energy. This is similar to witnessing the presence of Jesus Christ. To witness is to feel, not necessarily see. We may not be able to see Him, yet, we know that we are in His presence and believe that He is always with us. We can feel the energy that He provides as He guides us on our life journey.

For example, I'm sure at some point in your life, you have felt an uncomfortable feeling in your stomach when you were doing something that you didn't believe to be morally correct. This "feeling" isn't just an upset stomach from worrying or doing something that you know you shouldn't be doing. It's Jesus telling you that this is not the correct path for you. He is making His presence known so that we can feel Him with us. But then, Jesus will never forcefully guide us; He will simply make a suggestion (such as a "knot" in your stomach) and then let YOU make the decision.

Jesus knows the correct path for you to take, but He wants to see if you can trust Him to help you find it. There is a passage in the book of Acts Chapter 12, where Peter was arrested for being a Christian and was facing a public trial with the strong possibility of death. The night before Peter was scheduled to go to trial - while sleeping between two prison guards - an angel appeared, woke Peter up, removed his shackles, and told Peter to follow him out of the prison. But after removing Peter's chains, the angel said to him, "Put on your clothes and sandals."

This was our Lord saying, "I will help you find your path, but I am not going to do everything for you. I can remove your chains and walk you out of this prison, but YOU need to wake up, YOU need to stand up, YOU need to get dressed, and YOU need to follow me!"

Similarly, this is what you need to do when you find yourself in a dark place or seemingly impossible situation. You can ask Jesus for help and He will give you guidance, but YOU ultimately need to make the decision to stand up, make a change, and trust that He will never steer you wrong. You have the ability to make it out of any dark situation that you find yourself in. Look at Peter; he was one day away from his death, yet, his belief in Jesus and willingness to get up, get dressed, and walk out from the prison saved his life. Peter was freed from the shackles that once bound him. It's time for you to free yourself too!

There will be shackles in your life. At times, you will feel like you're chained and trapped, with no possibility of escaping. Whether it be a drug addiction, the loss of a close family member, or some other event that occurs in your life, YOU must trust that He will help you escape from those shackles. You will experience a plethora of miracles once you place your full trust into His hands.

Nothing is impossible until you start believing in impossibility. Again, look at Peter who seemed to be in an inescapable situation. He was sleeping between two guards, shackled, and in a prison, yet, he never lost his faith. This faith, along with his actions, led him to freedom. Just like Peter, you can escape. Believe in the Lord, follow His guidance, and put forth the work necessary. It takes your willingness to change and take action for you to escape the shackles.

10. Fighting Family

HOW STRONG IS your desire to achieve your goals in life? There will be days when you want to give up. You will become stressed, experience large amounts of anxiety, and, at times, it will feel like the world is against you. There were so many times in my life that I "should" have felt this way... according to those around me. There were so many times where I "should" have given up and taken an easier route. There were so many times where I "should" have thrown in the towel and taken the easy way out.

Outsiders will always attempt to provide an easy route, but the easy path doesn't always lead to a desirable outcome. If you limit yourself to the abilities and opinions of those around you, then you will find yourself trapped within their definition of "possible." Look at how many times my father defied "possibility" according to doctors' opinions.

Likewise, when my father was first diagnosed and doctors predicted his five-to-sixty day expiration date, the Dean of my law school suggested that I take the semester off from school to clear my mind. He didn't believe that it was possible for me to remain focused on my school work with everything that was going on back home. I remember him stating to me, "At least, lower your course load. Don't try to be Superman and have your grades suffer because you're attempting to do too much. I would hate to see you fail out of school due to the unfortunate circumstances you are currently dealing with."

I could have taken his advice, listened to his definition of what was possible, and either taken the time off, or dropped a couple of classes. However, I knew that I would be able to handle this situation.

Just like my father didn't fear the opinions of medical professionals, I didn't fear the challenge that was in front of me. So, instead of taking time off or dropping a couple of classes, I did the opposite. I enrolled into the school's business program to get my MBA in Sports Administration. I was able to do this since I knew that *possible* to me meant something different than *possible* to my Dean. "Something" told me that I could handle it and I knew "something" would help guide me through it all.

Not only did I graduate with both my Juris Doctorate and Master's in Business Administration degrees, I did so with flying colors. I was on the Dean's list in law school and never received a grade lower than a "B" in any of my business school courses. "Possibility" is a subjective term! What's possible for some may seem impossible to others and vice versa. You need to decide whether you wish to believe those around you and limit your definition, or if you plan to expand your definition beyond all doubters. I know that I want to continue to expand my definition because I truly feel like there is nothing that I cannot overcome, do, or succeed at.

Possibility is truly limitless. For example, on June 15, 2017, I received a phone call from my mother around 3:30pm. She told me that at 9:04am, my great-grandmother, who was 99 years of age, was pronounced dead. Furthermore, doctors attempted to resuscitate her for more than fifteen minutes without success. As the doctors were all exiting the room to begin their paperwork, one of the doctors grabbed my great-grandmother's hand for the last time.

Shocked at what she felt, the doctor yelled to her colleagues that she felt a pulse! "Somehow," after being dead and not having a pulse for approximately ten minutes, my great-grandmother came back to life! She defied what doctors deemed to be "impossible." The nurse at the hospital said she had never witnessed anything like that in more than twenty-five years of experience in her field.

Around 7:30pm that same evening, I Facetimed with my great-grandmother who was awake, alert, and eating ice cream in her bed. I was astonished and thanked Jesus countless times for placing me in this path to witness yet another miracle. It's incredible to think that my great-grandmother went on a trip to the Kingdom and back to her hospital bed all in the same day. Talk about a vacation!

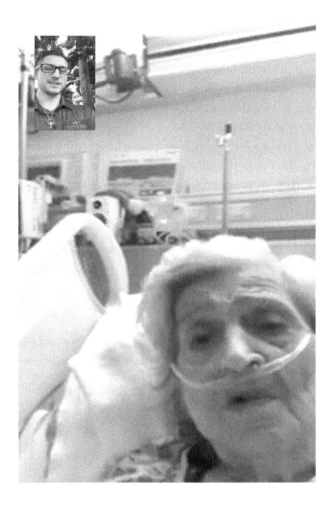

Curiously, my family asked her what she remembered during the time she was not with us on this earth. She stated that she remembered seeing a large door, and when she entered through the door, she saw her mother, father, and sister, all whom had predeceased her. After seeing that they were all comfortable and happy, she decided that it was time for her to return back to earth for a little bit longer. That night, she asked everyone in the hospital room to hold her hands and recite the Lord's Prayer with her. Then she began to apologize to every person in the room for something that she had done in the past; she asked everyone to please forgive one another for any resentment they were currently feeling.

Prior to hearing this story, I had the mistaken belief that you couldn't die and come back to life, since that was something only Jesus did. This "impossibility" was made possible that day. If you have a strong relationship with our Lord, then there is no such thing as impossible, since He has the power to make anything occur.

I want to encourage you the next time you are in an "impossible" situation to think of my great-grandmother. Think of how she overcame the one thing that many people attribute to impossibility – coming back from the dead. Now, when you re-evaluate your situation, you will see that there is a solution. There is a way for you to make it out of whatever current struggle you are facing. You just need to trust in Him and believe in yourself.

> "If you have a strong relationship with our Lord, then there is no such thing as impossible."

11. Trusting Trust

THROUGHOUT MY EVENTFUL journey called "life," I finally discovered a little thing known as "trust." We must learn to trust in the Lord and ourselves. There are too many people that I continue to come into contact with that don't trust the Lord or themselves. This lack of trust often leads to an unfulfilled life and contentment.

I don't believe that you should ever settle in life! There's always more for you to accomplish or do when walking with the Lord and trusting in your own capabilities. Finding the ability to trust in Jesus and myself has helped me overcome obstacles that many people never believed possible to achieve. I challenge you to ask yourself, if you will not trust in YOU, who will?

After my law school graduation, I started to prepare for the dreaded Bar exam. The majority of my colleagues put their entire life on halt for several months to prepare for the exam. They deactivated social media accounts, stopped working, placed their cellphones on "Do Not Disturb," and spent roughly twelve-to-sixteen hours studying in the library each day. My colleagues literally lived, breathed, and ate the law from May to July.

I, on the other hand, was different than most; well, like I have been my entire life. I continued to work full-time until two weeks prior to the exam. I kept all of my social media pages active since I saw social media as a free way to market my abilities and relationships in the hope of recruiting new athlete clients. I also registered to take my National Football League Players Association (NFLPA) Agent certification exam, which was scheduled just days prior to the Bar exam.

Most of my friends thought I was crazy. They thought I put too much on my plate and gave me a hard time for it. They told me to postpone my NFL agent exam and to focus on the Bar. They told me to stop working and spend the day in the library. They told me a lot of things, but, in reality, they didn't see my vision. They didn't know the plan that God had put in front of me. They didn't understand that the Bar exam wasn't important to me. It was important for me to continue working, continue building relationships, and to build a solid foundation for a bright future. Thus, I flew to Washington D.C. on July 19 for the NFLPA Agent Certification examination, which consisted of a two-day conference that was followed by the exam. On July 22, I caught a flight to Tampa, FL to take my Bar exam, which was scheduled for July 25th and 26th.

I had everything that I worked my entire life for come down to two exams that were set to occur just days apart. Yet, for "some reason," I remained calm throughout the entire process. I continued to show up to work every day and still found time to catch up with friends for dinner. I knew that I was more than capable of passing both exams and trusted that Jesus would help guide me through the waves that were quickly approaching.

When I arrived in Washington D.C., I quickly met up with several friends that I hadn't seen in years. It was amazing to see how well everyone was doing and how fast life had changed for everyone. But still, I knew that I needed to get focused to ensure that I passed my NFLPA examination, since this exam controlled my destiny in the sports world. This was my passion – my desire, and I truly believed it was my calling in life.

It's an amazing feeling when you discover your passion in life, but it's an even greater feeling when your passion puts you in a position to help others and witness them capture their dreams. I've always possessed a strong desire to help people and I also grew up playing sports, but I wasn't sure of how to combine the two of them. Being an NFL agent provided me the bridge to merge my two passions into one "super passion," – a feeling that I cannot even put into words. Thus, I was aware that after this exam, I would be able to help young men capture their dreams, ensure a successful living for themselves and their families, provide guidance, and be there for them whenever they needed a person to talk with.

I knew that this was a business of trust and relationships, but in order to gain someone else's trust, you must first be able to trust in yourself. For me, I was always an extremely confident individual. I always believed that I could accomplish anything that I set my mind to and trusted in my abilities, but I didn't realize that I couldn't fully trust myself until I found trust in "someone" much greater than any human on earth.

When I reflect back on all of the difficult situations that I was placed in, it still amazes me to think about the amount of "blind trust" that I had. What I mean by "blind trust" is that I trusted that "something" would get me through the difficult situation, but I was unaware of what that "something" or "someone" was. Now, because I'm aware of whom He is and how much power He possesses, my entire outlook on life has changed. I think that I finally have an understanding of how my father was able to stay so calm and confident during his gruesome battle with cancer. He trusted in his own abilities and the Lord's guidance.

DISTRACTIONS

Finding this trust helped me remain calm, confident, and aggressive during my preparation for my exams. I already knew that I was ready for the challenge, but I was also ready to show everyone around me how I could handle everything that was on my plate. Nothing was going to stop me from achieving these goals! But even when you finally become aware of Jesus' power and trust in Him, there will always be events that test the trust you that have.

Approximately one week prior to my scheduled departure for Washington D.C., the Dean of my law school called me on my cellphone while I was at the library, focusing on my preparations. He said, "Sam, I looked at your Bar preparation course online and it appears as if you haven't been completing your assignments." I explained to him that I was on a different schedule than most since I was working and preparing for my NFLPA agent certification exam at the same time.

When he heard those words come out of my mouth, you would have thought I had murdered someone. The panic and fear that was portrayed from his voice during that call shocked me. I was so confident in my own abilities that I assumed everyone around me would feel the same way – or, at least be supportive. Boy was I wrong.

My Dean said, "Sam, the Bar exam is a different animal than law school. Most people can't find the time to simply prepare for this exam, let alone prepare for two. I don't think this is a smart decision and I would highly discourage you from doing this." I was shocked. How could a Dean from my law school, who "wants to see me succeed," talk negatively toward me while I'm focused on accomplishing greatness? Why did he doubt me? I told him, "Don't worry about me. I am fine and I'm confident that I'm going to crush both of these exams. Please don't doubt me right now."

He responded with, "But this is different. This is just not a smart decision. Isn't there another option? Can't you take the NFL exam next year?" There was no other option in my mind and there did not need to be one.

I responded, "Why are you doubting me? Do you remember what happened the last time that you doubted me? Do you remember when my father was first diagnosed and you told me that I should probably drop out of school for the semester and start afresh the following year? Do you remember recommending for me to drop at least half of my classes to lighten my workload after I told you that I was not going to leave school? Do you remember recommending that I ask my professors to push my final exams back to a later date after my father passed away because you didn't think it would be possible to focus hard enough to pass my exams? Do you remember telling me to not try to be Superman? With all due respect, I'm not trying to be anyone. I AM SUPERMAN! Not only did I ignore your advice, I also added classes to my course load by achieving a second degree! Now, please, STOP DOUBTING ME."

This left the Dean shocked and speechless. He really didn't know how to respond and simply said, "I really hope to see your name on the passing list. Best of luck to you and I am pulling for you." I trusted in myself and believed that I could accomplish the "impossible." In life, things are only impossible if you limit yourself. I had zero plans on placing a limit on my abilities.

After completing my NFLPA Agent Certification exam, I went back to my Airbnb and packed for my early flight the next morning. It was time to change gears and focus on the Bar exam. My plan was to land in Tampa, catch an Uber to my hotel, and begin studying upon getting settled in. My plans changed in a hurry …

As I pulled into my hotel, I quickly noticed that this was actually a Motel and it was not in the greatest of areas. Still, I kept telling myself that everything would be okay and I simply needed to focus for the next couple of days so that I could pass this exam. When I first opened the door to my room, a strong odor caught my nose. The room smelled musty, like an old tent that had been left outside in a rainstorm, then baked in 90-degree weather for a few days. The furniture looked as if it had been there since the 1960's, the bed sheets were still dirty, the microwave looked as if a previous guest hit it with a baseball bat, the towels all had stains on them, and the TV barely turned on. I kept telling myself that I needed to remain calm and focused on the task at hand, and that Jesus would help guide me.

I decided to make the most of the situation, so I came up with a plan to eliminate one of the distractions – the musty smell. I looked on my iPhone for the closest store, which happened to be a little convenience store slightly over one mile away. This was the closest bar, restaurant, gas station, or store to my motel, so I took the walk to search for a candle or Febreze, but the store didn't have either in stock. So, I got resourceful and bought the next best thing – car air fresheners. I bought a package of the little tree-shaped yellow air fresheners and took them back to my room. I hung one on my front door and another in the bathroom. The air fresheners actually worked and I started to finally feel more comfortable in my new place.

That night, as I laid down for bed, I thanked Jesus for continuing to watch over me. I felt grateful that he blessed me with the opportunities that continued to come into my path. As I turned on my TV, I discovered that only one channel actually worked. It was a show about unsolved murder mysteries. Already feeling a little sketchy about the motel itself, I decided it was best to keep my TV off and I fell asleep.

The next morning, I was woken up by the sound of two men screaming outside of my door. I rolled over, looked at my phone, and saw that it was only 7:00am, so I decided that I was going to block out the noise and sleep for another thirty minutes. Then, about thirty seconds later, I heard someone yell the word, "gun."

I quickly jumped out of bed, made sure my door was locked, my lights were out, and the TV was shut off. I didn't want anyone to know that I was inside. Then a woman started screaming at the top of her lungs, "Don't do it. Get back here! Don't... he has a gun!" I didn't know what to think. I quickly texted my mother to inform her about the situation; I advised her not to call, since I didn't want to answer my phone. Someone yelled, "The cops are on their way." Then I heard a man's voice say, "**** no! You ain't gonna rob my a** at gun point. You ain't punkin me!" The woman started to scream again.

I just wanted to leave, get some coffee, and start studying for my exam. I had two days to get ready, so I ordered an Uber to come pick me up. Approximately ten minutes later, my Uber driver called me and said, "Sir, I am sorry, but I can't get anywhere near you. The police have the whole area blocked off and won't let me anywhere near where you are staying. There are cops everywhere! I'm not sure what's going on, but I am going to get out of here."

I told him to hold on and that I would walk to him. I packed up my bags, opened the front door, and saw five police officers standing there, hiding behind vehicles and these large pillars that were a part of the motel's foundational structure, with their guns drawn. One of the officers waved his gun at me and said, "Get back inside, lock your door, and get down." I quickly shut my door, ran into my bathroom, and laid down on the ground behind my bathtub in case a stray bullet found its way into my room. For "some reason," I didn't fear the situation. I remained calm and felt protected, even though I was unsure of what was going on outside.

Finally, approximately forty-five minutes later, the police officers told me that it was okay to come outside. An older gentleman, who was staying in the room adjacent to mine, told me that he opened his door at one point and saw a bloody man running across the parking lot with a chain wrapped around his fist. At this point, I went to the main office of the motel and asked for a refund. I couldn't afford to have these distractions occur on a daily basis and feared that I would miss my exam if I was unable to leave my parking lot due to a similar situation. Thankfully, they provided me with a full refund without much of a hassle and I found a much nicer hotel a few miles down the road.

By trusting in Jesus, I was able to stay calm in an otherwise frantic situation. I trusted that He would guide me. He knew that the motel would be a distraction to me; it was, from the moment I entered the property. Thus, He orchestrated the armed robbery the following morning to enable me to upgrade to a much nicer and calmer hotel right down the road. He always trusted in me and by seeing my trust in Him, He rewarded me with comfort – both physical and spiritual.

In life, there will be many dark and difficult situations that we face on a daily basis. By learning to trust in both the Lord and ourselves, we will be able to continue to march forward through these difficult times. Adversity makes a person stronger, but trust can make a human fearless! By trusting in Jesus, I fear no man, situation, or event, since I know He is watching over and guiding me.

I was able to turn my blind trust into something much more powerful through the recognition of our Savior's power. When you finally become aware of the trust that you have in both yourself and Him, it will empower you to turn impossible into "I'M POSSIBLE!" Notice how much of a difference that little separation of letters can make. Now, create that same separation between yourself and others because their vision and perspective on life should not impact yours. View reality through your own lens. Possible only becomes impossible when you set limitations.

12. Being an NFL Agent

MY CAREER ISN'T your average 9:00am to 5:00pm job. When most people hear about what I do for a living, they think it's the coolest job in the world. They think that I'm some form of celebrity or a multi-millionaire. The reality is, I do have the coolest job in the world! I get to help young men become successful human beings... both on the football field and in life. There's nothing more satisfying than helping someone achieve a life-long dream, which can also create financial security for them and their family for the rest of their lives.

Most people don't see the struggle that it takes to work in sports. As I talked about earlier, my entry point into the sports industry was unique. I went from volunteering at a charitable foundation to securing my dream job with an employer that initially told me "No." However, the struggle didn't stop because I was hired by a sports agency. In fact, it was just getting started.

When I started working with Neostar, my salary was $0. I literally worked 50-100 hours a week for no pay. But that's the sports industry. You "eat what you kill," so to speak. If you aren't bringing in business, then you aren't making any money. Yet, I saw value elsewhere. I believed that it was more valuable networking, learning the insides of the sports business industry, and making a name for myself than it was making a fast dollar. I knew that I was more than qualified, but there were a ton of things that I needed to learn.

One of the first things that I learned while working in the sports industry is that it's all about who knows you, not who you know. Relationships are everything and can be more valuable than money itself. This is what gets you in the door, or a seat at the table, so to speak. Without relationships, it's extremely difficult to do anything. This is where working with Ralph Stringer and Marvin Demoff became invaluable. Ralph and Marvin have relationships all around the country and have worked with most, if not all, of the NFL sponsors, team owners, and general managers during their more than 70 years' worth of combined experience, working in the sports industry.

This gave me a big advantage as a young agent since I was able to piggyback off of these relationships as I also developed my own.

Additionally, Ralph and Marvin represent one of the most iconic and credible names in all of sports, Dan Marino. This gave me instant credibility when sparking conversations with NFL teams, prospective client's parents, and pretty much anyone else working in the sports industry.

Now, don't get me wrong, even with having the backing of people like Ralph and Marvin, I still had to show up and make those connections myself. I had to spark random conversations everywhere I went and made a lot of my connections while spending weeks at the NFL Combines, All-Star games, or cold-emailing team personnel to initiate conversations. But that's what it takes to make it in one of the most cut-throat and competitive industries in the world. You have to be able to put your ego aside, be vulnerable, and sell yourself to everyone around you. Time is money, so, make yourself valuable!

I can't even begin to tell you how many times I would walk up to introduce myself and people would walk away, say they were busy, or just didn't give me the time of day. I've been denied more times than I can count. Yet, I kept coming back. I kept fighting and kept showing up at every event possible. If I had the money, then I was getting on an airplane and networking my ass off. It was that simple.

The second lesson that I learned is that it's very expensive to get started in the athlete representation business. To put it into perspective, when a college athlete decides to sign with an agent to help him through the NFL Draft and NFL Combine process, the agent is the person or company that typically covers all of the bills. You may ask how expensive that can really get since the entire NFL Draft process is only four to five months. Well, for a mid-round draft pick (4th or 5th round) this bill can range from $20,000 to $60,000. That's right … $20,000 to $60,000 that you have to pay out of pocket before ever seeing a penny in return. Let's not even get started on a 1st round draft prospect.

A lot of agents will pay for everything for the athlete from their last collegiate game until he is drafted by an NFL team. This includes weight training, position specific training, massages, therapy,

Wonderlic preparations, interview training, yoga, housing, vehicle, monthly stipends, food, nutritionists, flights, hotels, family dinners, additional recovery treatments, etc. This doesn't even include the money you spent recruiting the athlete by taking flights, game tickets, hotels, rental cars, gas, meals for yourself on the road, etc. Needless to say, it is expensive to start out and actually compete in this industry!

When I started, I was a recent law school graduate with no money. My mother didn't have money to give me, I couldn't get approved for a loan, and I wasn't making a salary. Yet, I possess traits that a lot of people who have the money in the industry don't – HEART, WILL-POWER, and PERSISTENCE. I will never quit fighting. Therefore, I had to get creative when I signed my first couple of clients. I'll never forget my first draft class.

I signed three total athletes all from very respected Universities. None of the three athletes had "draftable" grades (meaning teams did not project that my clients would be drafted by a team during the NFL Draft) from the scouts that I spoke with, yet, I had to start somewhere. I ended up partnering with a law firm in Pittsburgh - a story for another day - who agreed to put up most of the money necessary to train the athletes, in return for a percentage of what the agency makes on the athlete's NFL contract. The way it works for most agencies is that the agent will pay for all of the training costs upfront and then make it back by taking a percentage of the athlete's NFL contract. The NFL Players Association implemented a system to make 3% the maximum an agent can charge on an athlete's team contract.

I'll create a hypothetical instance here to explain things a little easier. You sign an athlete and figure out that it will cost $20,000 to get that athlete trained and ready for the NFL Combine and the NFL Draft. You are charging your client 3%. Your client doesn't get drafted, but signs with a team as an Undrafted Free Agent for a rookie minimum contract, making $610,000 in year one. If your client makes the team and is on the active roster for every game, then you can charge your client $18,300 in year one, which doesn't even pay back your initial investment, let alone allow you to make a profit. If your client does not make a team's active roster, then you cannot charge your client anything and you lose your $20,000 investment. That is a risk that not many people are willing to make.

Now, back to my first three clients. When they decided to sign with me, I was living alone in a two-bedroom apartment in Davie, FL. One of my three clients lived in the Miami area while the other two were from out of the state. After looking at several different NFL Combine and Pro Day preparation training facilities, we collectively decided that the three athletes were going to train together at a top facility located in Davie, FL.

Immediately, it enabled one of my clients to continue living at home, and he had a nice vehicle to drive, so, that eliminated two large expenses. For the two out of state clients, I gave up both bedrooms in my apartment and decided that I would sleep on the couch for the next three to four months while they trained. My day now revolved around them. I left my house every morning to drop my clients off at the training facility, went to my office to work, picked them up when they were finished with their training for the day, would head to a coffee shop to continue my work, and then came home to sleep on the couch. It was a tough couple of months. I felt like a stranger in my own home since I was the only person who didn't have his own bedroom. I even packed most of my clothes into a suitcase so that I could change each morning in the living room and not have to enter one of the bedrooms.

After about two months, I realized that staying in the same apartment was not going to work for anyone. There just wasn't enough space, and if I slept on the couch, then they wouldn't have a living room to enjoy. I called my friend Vinnie (who now works with me) and asked if I could stay with him for the next couple of months. Luckily, he allowed me to stay on his couch. The only issue became that I was now staying 20 miles from my apartment, so I needed to find a new way to get my clients to their training sessions and anywhere else they needed to go. So, I decided to let them borrow my car for the remaining months, while I took Ubers anywhere that I needed to go. It was cheaper this way, since I only had to Uber once or twice a day. My clients, on the other hand, needed to get to/from training, go to a different place for recovery, and go anywhere else they wanted to go.

I'm not going to lie, those two to three months felt like an entire year, but it was a learning experience that I'll never forget. I was determined to get my foot in the door anyway possible, and wanted to make a real name for myself in the sports industry. This sacrifice was just my first step.

The NFL Draft came and passed. None of my clients signed with a team immediately. Then I was finally able to secure a tryout for one of my clients who made the team's initial 90-man roster. He bounced around the NFL for a few months, but was never really able to stick. When you're in the industry for any period of time, you quickly learn that NFL really means "Not For Long."

I'll admit it, I was a little discouraged. I believed that I was going to have a first-round draft pick year in my first year. I could have never envisioned that I wouldn't even have a client on a team.

The next year, I decided that I was going to come out swinging and recruit only high-profile college athletes for the NFL Draft. I set up meetings around the country with athletes and their families, utilizing every angle possible to get my foot in the door. There was one athlete, in particular that I really wanted to have as a client. He played for Florida State University and was one of the best defensive players in all of college football. Thus, I made it my mission to spend the most time and energy on him!

I did all of my research and found out that one of our retired clients was his favorite athlete while growing up. More so, I took it a step further and made it a mission to learn everything that I could about his family. I knew where he went to high school, how many siblings he had, where his mother worked, his high school football coach, what his favorite food was, why he chose to attend Florida State, etc. I became good friends with his mother, sister, and brother – all of whom I still communicate with today.

I attended nearly every home game that Florida State had that year, making the seven-hour drive a nearly weekly routine. At this point, Vinnie was now working with me, so we would split the drive to Tallahassee, which made it a lot more doable. Meanwhile, we still had our work to do for our existing clients, so, we had to make as trips as short as possible. Furthermore, we had to stay within our very tight budget.

There were several occasions where we would leave Miami early in the morning, arrive in Tallahassee just after lunch-time, go to the team hotel to see the athlete's family, attend the 8pm football game, meet with the athlete and his family after the game, hit the road around 1am, and drive through the night to get to a Dolphins home game the next morning. During those trips, we would drive straight to the stadium, take a 30 to 40-minute nap in the car, and be down on the field for pre-game workouts by 10am. It was a grind, but Vinnie and I enjoyed it.

We experienced a lot during those trips to Tallahassee. Between flat tires, nearly running out of gas, staying in a Motel that had blood on the sheets, and renting an Airbnb that was actually a person's garage, we both have stories that will last a lifetime.

Unfortunately, the athlete decided to sign with a different agency, but it definitely wasn't because of a lack of effort. His final decision was between me and another agent. I hate second place. In reality, it's a blessing that things worked out the way that they did. I learned a lot and, in that moment, God knew that I wasn't ready for the task at hand. I was pretty much single-handedly doing the work at that point. Ralph was no longer registered as a Certified Contract Advisor with the NFLPA, Marvin wasn't fully in the picture yet, and Vinnie had just started in the business. I'm sure we would have made a lot of mistakes with a very high-profile athlete.

It's incredible how Jesus constantly opens doors for those who trust His guidance. There were countless times that I wanted to quit. Shoot, after my first NFL Draft I wanted to just call it quits and start looking for a different career path. I was broke, couldn't pay my bills, had 0 active NFL clients, felt lost in an industry full of sharks, and just didn't know what to do next. But if I would have quit, I would have missed out on so many memories. I would have missed out on having my first ever client drafted! I would have missed out on Super Bowls, flying around the country on private jets, and helping young men battle adversity.

I always remembered my father's saying, "God gives his strongest soldiers the most difficult battles." I knew that I was in one of the most competitive industries, yet, I also knew that I was one of God's strongest soldiers. I believe that Jesus put Vinnie, Marvin and Ralph into my life for a reason, and I'm excited to see what the future has in store for all of us.

13. Find Your Light

IN LIFE, NO matter what path you ultimately decide to pursue, you are destined to experience storms. There will be times where no matter how much you prepare for the storm, it will be more powerful than you could have ever imagined. My violent storm was my father's battle with cancer, his death, finishing two degrees, and working full time. These were all occurring simultaneously! Yet, I took all of my fears and emotions and turned them into energy. I was able to find the bright light that helped guide me through the storm. I may not have reached my final destination just yet, but I know that I am on the correct path. I'm sure that more storms will approach, but I'm ready! I know that our Lord gives His strongest soldiers the most difficult tasks, and I'm ready to face them.

How are you going to respond the next time you're trapped in a storm? How will you react when your path is blocked? What will you do when things do not go the way that you plan? How will you handle a situation when you see a Savable Other start to take the forbidden path? Hopefully, you turn all of those negatives into positive energy.

Hopefully, you do not waste the most precious thing that you have – TIME! As difficult as it may be, try to put your selfish emotions aside and figure out a solution to your impediment. I'm not suggesting that you should never express emotions and that I'm an emotionless human being – that would be a lie, as I cry all of the time. But I am saying that there isn't time to feel sorry for yourself. There isn't time to keep running on that treadmill of excuses because you need to get back on your path.

This is how I use my time:

Think about your future.

Increase your chances of success.

Make your own path, don't wait for one to be created.

Embark on your journey with Christ. You're never alone.

How are you going to utilize your time?

CPSIA information can be obtained
at www.ICGtesting.com
Printed in the USA
BVHW071931100122
625896BV00009B/292/J

9 781977 248527